Praise for Bat

M000227664

It has been said, "you are in a problem or just left one or headed toward one." In other words, in this thing called life, all of us will have battles to fight and if you haven't had any as of now, keep living. Nate Battle, author, and speaker, in a courageous and transparent way, gives us a battle plan to help us navigate the storms of life we will face time and time again. I found it instructive, informative and inspiring. This book provides a guide to live your life Victoriously.

— Les Brown Motivational Speaker, Author of *It's Not Over Until You Win*

"Nate has a gift of helping and mentoring others in a way I've never seen or experienced before. His book, BATTLE, represents his gift, as it is uniquely inspirational, insightful, and powerful. His book is a blessing because now he will be able to touch and help so many others, like he did for me, truly changing their lives forever, for the better. Nate truly does have a gift. He has this way of saying something that others have told me a million times, yet it clicks when he says it."

— Megan D.

"Nate has nailed it with the book! Life can be a constant set of battles and too many think they're in it alone. This book is a reminder your not and a tool to help you get through those tough days."

— Tamara E.

"Nate is the kind of person you immediately feel you've known for years. His positive energy is contagious! Constantly carrying a smile on his face, he always has good advice, a kind word and a unique way to make your day better! Reading this book was like chatting with a friend for hours about life, challenges, laughter, and tears with simplicity and comfort. This is not only a book that motivates people... This book "pushed" me to fight for better opportunities for me and my family with an outstanding courage and inexplicable certainty that better things were about to happen. And they did! You see yourself in this book and feel there's a piece of you in those lines! Truly inspiring and motivational."

— Helena C.

This is REALLY good! Definitions are excellent! Includes the research many would have to do in tandem with the reading. The material is personal and believable. So many believers struggle in these areas. This book puts language around so many feelings I had. It also reminds me of a place of peace that must be maintained for me to avoid those pitfalls. This book is for anyone but especially believers because the attacks on their minds seems more intense if they plan to do anything purposeful. I like how Nate used his experience. Brilliant and unfortunately, by God's grace, I know all of this came out of his own pain. But I'm thankful he willed himself to a place of submission to God's will by using this material to bless, encourage and liberate people. On behalf of all those people and me, thank you.

— Sheila M.

"Through Nate's journey, he arms us with itemized tools to fight the battles of both the mind and spirit while demonstrating he is a brother in arms to ANYONE who will accept nothing but victory in the battlefields of life."

— VIV C.

I've been reading all weekend. Thank God and Nate Battle. Yesterday I read about focusing on what you want, not only what "you don't want " in order to get a proper and more positive outlook. Can I say PROFOUND!

— Virginia D.

"I look at Nate as a honest person. Someone who has been through some tough times, as we all have, but does not quit. A very good person to get trustworthy advice from whether it's what you want to hear or not. It comes from within to help you, not judge or make you feel bad. A genuine person indeed."

—Toya S.

This book is an archive of some of the best teachings I have had in my career thus far."

— Bryan W.

BATTLE

ENDURANCE

How You Can Be Someone
Who Never Quits and Gives
Everything You Have To Give

NATE BATTLE

Published by BC Press

ISBN 13: *978-1-932707-04-5*

Library of Congress Catalog Number: 2016915678

First Printing, 2016

www.battlecoaching.com

This book is dedicated to my wife, Michelle, who is first and foremost my best friend, as well as my life partner and pillar of support.

And to my children, Nadia, Courtney, and T'rone, the joys and purpose of my life.

To my parents, Burnie and Bessie, who have demonstrated fearless courage and strength.

CONTENTS

FOREWORD

My intent is for you to use this book as a practical survival guide, a handy reference to refer to over and over. When you need to know that you are not alone on the journey, know that others have gone through it before or are experiencing what you are facing, perhaps at this very moment.

I share parts of my journey and the journeys of those whose paths I have been honored to cross. The names have been changed in the stories I have included to protect identities. I use these examples to affirm you are not crazy (well, not in the clinical sense) and that what you are feeling is natural. I use them to uplift, inspire, and, most of all, encourage you to go on and live your best life.

A crisis is not unlike Florida termites: it is not a matter of if but when you will face one. Being confronted with a crisis is inevitable in life. Unfortunately, the more we hope to try and accomplish, the more crises we face. The challenges become even greater as we get closer to reaching a plateau.

Personally, I have endured a significant number of crisis situations in my life. I've shared some of them throughout this book. These are experiences that are not unique to me; I'm certain that I am not the only one who has faced the challenges I have.

This book is about surviving crises and how to endure during them. While I may be unique as an individual, there's really nothing unique about my experiences. We all experience crisis in some form or another. Some of us have the opportunity to experience crises one at a time, while others may face multiple crises at the same time. But regardless, at some point in our lives, we all face a crisis.

Where you read my story, insert your own, your adversity, your crisis. Make the experience yours. It will help as you apply the method and approach for how to get the best out of each situation, rather than letting it get the best of you.

What Is this Book You Are Holding?

The following pages contain my story and experience. I do not claim to have cornered the market on facing and dealing with adversity. As you read through the pages that follow, you may find in some cases that your crisis is eerily similar, while in others yours might be entirely different. In both instances, if you are holding this book, my guess is you can relate. My only aim is to share my journey in the hope that even one person will gain insight (and maybe a few nuggets) that will encourage them to continue. I want to inspire others to stay the course on the path toward discovering a better version of themselves. Having battled the storms of life myself, I want to motivate others to not give up but to endure while finding peace in the midst of crisis.

Crisis and Endurance Defined

Dictionary.com defines the word *crisis* as:

1. a stage in a sequence of events at which the trend of all future events, especially for better or for worse, is determined; turning point.

2. a condition of instability or danger, as in social, economic, political, or international affairs, leading to decisive change.

3. a dramatic emotional or circumstantial upheaval in a person's life.

The *Oxford Dictionary* definition states:

1. a time of intense difficulty or danger.

2. a time when a difficult or important decision must be made.

3. the turning point of a disease when an important change takes place, indicating either recovery or death.

The *Merriam-Webster Dictionary* definition of *crisis* is:

1. a paroxysmal attack of pain, distress, or disordered function

2. the decisive moment

3. an unstable or crucial time or state of affairs in which a decisive change is impending;

especially: one with the distinct possibility of a highly undesirable outcome

a situation that has reached a critical phase

Crises can have different meanings depending on your level of tolerance or adverseness to the situation. In other words, what might appear to be a crisis of not having the right pair of shoes to match a particular style of outfit for work may be of little consequence to the person without a job, or with a job but no feet.

While that example might be a little extreme, it is intended to point out that even situations that clearly fall within the definition of a crisis may have a different level of impact on the individual experiencing them.

For one person, material stability may have a higher importance than love or relationships, while others might appreciate the quality of their relationships and human interaction above all else.

Regardless, if we are human, we will face crises—in fact, many of them—in our lifetimes.

I recall a particular situation that I would consider my own definition of crisis when I worked for a tech company before the dot.com bubble burst in the late 1990s. We experienced wild growth while enjoying high levels of interest from potential investors. The leading-edge business model of this tech company was unprecedented at the time. We received tremendous attention from large corporations, one even investing in rather than acquiring us. It was commonplace to have client prospects more interested in how they could get in on the IPO than on the highly appealing service offering. It felt like a sure a thing. The stock was predicted to perform similarly to Cisco's stock once the company went public. I recall the CEO communicating that based on anticipated performance projections; the receptionist with 500 shares would become a millionaire. I had invested in nearly 30,000 shares of stock by scraping, scrounging, and borrowing every penny I could to purchase them.

I worked tirelessly with the company, putting in all-nighters and traveling overseas for weeks at a time. Whenever I would feel fatigued or question why I was doing this, I would bring up a spreadsheet created with different stock performance projections, which displayed the millions I would make after the IPO.

Shortly before the company was to go public, I resigned and started a non-profit in anticipation of being able to pursue philanthropic endeavors.

The tech market at the time was hotter than ever with

soaring stock prices. The sustained growth showed no signs of slowing. I often wondered why we didn't go public sooner but was thrilled to see that we had finally set a date and were on the IPO docket.

I watched and waited with great anticipation, counting the days. Minor volatility began to appear in the market with down days, but we all thought it was just a short-term anomaly.

About two weeks before the IPO, the tech bubble burst. The stock markets crashed—hard. Widespread panic and investor withdrawal furthered the collapse of the tech market.

I remained hopeful even as I watched the slow and painful ebbing away of tech stocks, hoping each day for good news, but each day the news got worse.

The much-anticipated IPO date came and went with deafening silence. I continued to watch in hopeful anticipation or hopeless denial. Days turned into weeks, which turned into months, until it was evident that there would be no IPO.

Instead of becoming a multi-millionaire, I eventually ended up starting over, from scratch, from nothing. This was all too familiar territory as it was one of three times I had been tracking toward becoming a millionaire but instead ended up starting over.

There are no words to describe adequately the tsunami of emotions I experienced from this.

In the pages that follow, I will share what I've learned about identifying the typical stages we may go through in the battles of life. We might experience them all or just a few. Each of them may last for a long time or only for a brief encounter. Following the stages, I offer three phases of coping with and enduring a crisis. I hope you find them helpful.

Dictionary.com defines the word *endurance* as:

1. the fact or power of enduring or bearing pain, hardships, etc.
2. the ability or strength to continue or last, especially despite fatigue, stress, or other adverse conditions; stamina
3. lasting quality; duration
4. something endured, as a hardship; trial

The Oxford Dictionary Press definition of *endurance* states:

1. the ability to endure an unpleasant or difficult process or situation without giving way
2. the capacity of something to last or to withstand wear and tear

The *Merriam-Webster Dictionary* definition of *endurance* is:

1. the ability to do something difficult for along time
2. the ability to deal with pain or suffering that continues for a long time
3. the quality of continuing for a long time

Simply put, we endure during a crisis—or two or three. In carefully examining the definition of endurance, it encompasses:

- adversity
- trials
- challenges
- all manner of crises

These are the situations that require us to use every last bit of strength that we can muster—sometimes we didn't even know we had it in us. The obstacles, enemies, and challenges we face test us and help define our character.

Our ability to endure—in other words, how long we can press forward—is based on our stamina, strength, pain threshold, and courage.

Stages of Endurance in Crisis

We may experience many stages of endurance in crisis. The following are what I believe to be the most common stages people go through. That is not to say you will go through all of them in your own journey. Nor am I saying that you will go through them to the same degree that others might. The primary intent of sharing this is to affirm that:

A. *you are not alone.*
B. *you are not crazy for feeling the way you do or for having the feelings you have.*
C. *you should avoid making matters worse by being hard on yourself or beating yourself up for being human.*

A crisis can affect each of us differently based on our uniqueness. I have learned over the years that if you want to handle a challenge efficiently, you should start by identifying its components by name. Moving targets are the toughest to hit. Know what you are battling.

These stages help put a name to the experience.

Each stage provides insight as to what you may feel or experience. The goal is to move past the stage once you have fully identified with the experience and the related emotion(s). In short, the categories are intended as places along the path, not as destinations. Visit if you must, but then move on.

Initial Stages

"Did that just happen?!"

"Is this seriously happening to me?!"

These are typical reactions during the first moments of a crisis.

SHOCK AND DISBELIEF

Those reactions remind me of a (rare) hot summer day growing up in Minnesota. I was driving down a side street one sunny afternoon on my way to work at my dad's office.

There I was scooting along in my florescent orange VW station wagon, which I would later learn was only held together by its fresh paint job. There was no music playing from the empty hole in the dashboard where the aftermarket stereo once lived before thieves had helped themselves to it.

I was going the speed limit while daydreaming about my plans for after I got off work. All of a sudden there appeared a sturdy, older sedan heading into the intersection in front of me. Its faded earth-tone color blended in with the dried-out brown grass behind it. By the time the other driver and I saw each other, it was too late. Perhaps each of us had thought the other was going to stop or slow down since neither of us had a stop sign. I recall feeling alarm at an imminent collision as I slammed on the brakes and tried to slow down on nearly bald tires.

Screeeeeeeechhhhh . . . BOOM!

What quickly followed was utter disbelief:

"Did that just really happen?!"

I got my answer quickly when I realized I had T-boned the other car; my now-throbbing knee provided further proof, having been jammed into the metal dashboard. Thankfully that new and small space provided just the right obstacle to prevent my body from being ejected through the windshield.

If you've ever been in an accident (or crash as we call them now) and were fortunate enough to remain conscious, you may recall the surreal shock. Questions of disbelief fire off in your brain, trying to process what just happened.

Your inciting incident might be dropping your new phone or a freshly baked cake, the loss of your job or the betrayal of a close friend. It may be when you find out someone borrowed your identity and all of the money that went with it. Perhaps it is the news of having lost a loved one. Regardless, the first moments are shocking.

ANGER

Now enter the next character in the play: Anger. Once we get past the initial shock and disbelief, realizing that this thing is, in fact, a real thing, well, that's when anger sets in. One of our more common reactions to a crisis is anger. The risk of bitterness, despair, and being in a rut occurs. Alan Lampkin is best known for the quote: "A rut is a grave with no ends." Anger is a very negative energy.

You may be able to relate to some of these expressions:

"Look what you did to my car!"

"What . . . what?! You can't lay me off! After all that I have done for this company?"

"Oh no, you cannot be for real, you're messing around with them? How could you? After all that we've been through together!"

"What do you mean he was better qualified for the position?"

"Those thieves took everything! What did I do to deserve this?"

"She's gone—why her? Why now! Why not someone else?!"

I could go on, but you get the idea. Depending on your experience, you may have been seething in anger, with the veins in your face about to burst along with Fourth of July fireworks exploding in your head all at once. Fighting to maintain control, you are sometimes unsuccessful. When you regain your composure, you are just plain mad.

"Now what?" No harm in experiencing the emotion;

however, like with the drop on a roller coaster, we are not supposed to remain there. Go ahead, get mad in the moment. Feel the anger for a brief time. Experience the upset, and then let it go. What's that saying? "Cry a river, build a bridge, and get over it!"

If we spend too much time being angry, anger can lead to more bitterness and despair and cause us to become further destructive. As a polar opposite of positivity, negativity will repel the very thing you lost and desire to have back—that peace you had before the crisis.

Experiencing anger is natural; staying angry is not, and it serves no purpose in the long term. Think of anger as a paper towel you use to clean up a spill. You certainly wouldn't hold on to the used paper towel after you were done with it, would you?

Imagine using the paper towel to wipe up the spill and then reusing it again and again. The paper towel would become rank, and even more quickly if used on spilled milk. We can become as sour and foul smelling as that filthy reused paper towel by trapping in anger and letting it seep into everything we do and say.

FEAR

Psychologists tell us that while there are different types of fear, they mostly fall into a few primary categories: fear of death, fear of pain or injury, fear of loss or of being trapped, fear of abandonment or rejection, fear of being humiliated or failure, and, our favorite, fear of the unknown.

Real crisis can invoke one or more of these. The lingering crisis has a way of building up fear to crushing levels. Over time, we can experience that type of suffocating fear and anxiety that feels like constant pressure. It can feel like a heavy weight pushing down on you. Sometimes it may seem as if it surrounds and engulfs you as you walk. It pushes down on you when you lie down, with equal force pushing up underneath you. There is no escaping it. You feel pressure closing in on you from every side, angle, surface, and limb, from your eyes, even from every hair follicle.

Medical professionals divide fear into two categories: healthy and unhealthy. We can presume that healthy fear is what helps us perform superhuman feats like lifting cars off people to save their lives, or perhaps winning a gold medal. The unhealthy fear almost always has to do with things imagined—either actually occurring or that may happen in the future. In both cases, however, neither currently exists— or at least not outside of our minds. I will cover this topic in more depth later in the book, including ways to deal with it. But for now, let's just go with the premise that unhealthy fear is the type that is mostly not real.

One of my favorite ways to relax is ocean kayaking. Being out there in the vast, open waters always helps me wash away worry and strife, at least for a while. Preferring to be as far from shore as possible, I paddle out past the shelf, where the depth of the ocean floor drops by over 1,000 feet!

After I shared tales of my excursions with co-workers, they cautioned that there were sharks in the area. I was cavalier in my dismissal of their warnings until they showed me videos and news stories of sharks; one showed thousands of them migrating to warmer waters just a couple of years prior.

Still, I continued to venture out past the shelf during my weekend outings. Occasionally I looked into the ocean water . . . you know, just in case. One time as I glanced down into the water, I noticed a large school of fish swimming around in tight formation. They swirled around me on one side and then around the back and to the other side. I became even more intrigued as I watched their highly synchronized movements, and I wondered what they were after. As the dark mass came closer, I realized that it was not a school but in fact a single fish, a big fish, a huge fish. As it continued to swirl and probe around my kayak, it got closer and swam right up to my left side. It came up near the surface and quickly inverted itself so I could see its underbelly—it was a shark!

As I began to head back, I imagine the view from the shore must have resembled one of those cartoons where the character shrieks and starts paddling so fast that he leaves the surface of the water, becoming airborne; at least that's how it felt. I glanced back once to see if the shark was still following and got a glimpse of the dark spot. I kept paddling, frantically declaring in my head:

"If I'm going out, I'm going out fighting!"

I continued to paddle ferociously, my heart pounding and my eyes focused on the sandy beach in front of me as I braced for the anticipated bump to my kayak.

As I got closer to safety with no attack, I began to plot:

"If I can just get close to shore, I can stand up and fight this man-eating bully beast."

As I approached the shore, I was relieved to see the lifeguard headed toward me. I was hopeful that regardless of what happened next, I would have some reinforcements if need be. Finally making it to shallow waters, I breathed a huge sigh of relief, got out of my kayak, and began dragging it ashore. The lifeguard greeted me with a scolding. "The boat launch and dock areas are down there. You are not supposed to come ashore here in the beach area."

Speechless and still in shock over what happened, I didn't get a chance to tell him there was a shark out there, as he had turned and walked away his gait broadcasting his satisfaction in having completed his important duty for the day.

A few weeks later, I finally worked up the nerve to venture back out into the ocean for more kayaking. Paddling along, I heard the lifeguards blowing their whistles. I disregarded the first few whistles, attributing their use to notifying some kid who probably swam out too far. I finally realized why they kept blowing their whistles when one of the lifeguards ran down to the shoreline frantically waving his arms to get my attention. They had been trying to tell me that I was too close to shore!

After my close call, I could not get the thought of that shark out of my mind. I later learned it had been a bull shark only about five or so feet in length. The experience of seeing it still lingered in my head.

From that point on, every time I went out I almost constantly looked for any dark mass in the water, visualizing every patch of seaweed, cloud reflection, and shadow I saw as a shark. I probably imagined quite a few along the way.

I use this story to illustrate how the trauma of a dramatic event can play into our perceptions. I'm not talking about a full-blown phobia here—an irrational fear, although misguided perceptions left unchecked could certainly get there.

Yes, it is prudent to be cautious and perhaps best to avoid paddling a mile out and hanging a supply of freshly cut raw meat over the side of the boat while dripping blood into the water. There was no need to worry that I might summon a great white from the depths of the ocean and have mini panic attacks with every paddle. More people die from falling coconuts, mosquito bites, and selfies than from shark attacks.

What I was doing in my mind was allowing fear to rob me of the peaceful, relaxing, and fulfilling experience that came from my weekend kayaking. It turned into more of a chore, like an exercise, than the enjoyment I had intended it to be. I could do just as well at a gym or even in my living room. How often do we miss out on something beautiful, breathtaking, or even just worth pausing to take in because of fear? How many times have we replayed what was or what might be, rather than focusing on what is?

I learned an interesting tidbit from the folks at National Geographic. By their estimates, you have a 1 in 63 chance of dying from the flu and a 1 in 3,700,000 chance of being killed by a shark during your lifetime.

Despair: Crisis Hell

You know those dreams when you've broken out in a cold sweat and are curled up in a ball writhing in pain? The ones where your heart is racing, and you have the chills and feel nauseated, like someone punched you in the stomach? It is perhaps one of the most overwhelming and hopeless feelings in the world. Then suddenly you wake up and realize it was all a dream. "It's not true!" you excitedly say to yourself, relieved that all is well.

Now, remember those times when you feel this same way, yet when you wake, it's true. That feeling, the depths of despair, only begins to tell the story of crisis hell.

DAYMARE, NOT NIGHTMARE

When it's only a nightmare, we can't wait to wake up and get out of bed, getting as far away from that terrible place as we can. We are filled with relief knowing that it was only a dream, a nightmare. We separate ourselves from the horror as quickly as possible. But when it's not a bad dream and is actually happening, either in our imagination or in stark reality, we prefer the opposite. We'd like to stay in bed and never get out if possible, wishing we could just curl up and hope the pain away, trying to turn it into a nightmare or just make it go away. We long for the world to stop, if only for a while, so we can regain the strength we need to go on, but which we simply do not have at that moment.

That place is called *crisis hell*. It feels empty and hopeless. Absent of joy. Dark, damp, hostile, and the last place on earth we ever want to be. That is until we realize that it is the doorway to where we want to go.

MIND ON FIRE

You know those nights, in the heat of a crisis, when you just can't sleep? You want to, but you just can't because of the stress. It is the type of stress where your body is physically exhausted, perhaps even squirming in agony, but your mind is still going 100 mph—you feel almost like an engine at full throttle, whirring with thoughts swirling around at warp speed. You feel like your mind is on fire. You try to tune out the constant and deafening noise and try to get at least a little sleep, but the anxiety-inducing thoughts rapidly fly all around and are just too much to ignore.

WRONG PLACE

One of the telltale signs that we need to make a change is when we look at ourselves honestly in the mirror and don't recognize the reflection we see. It might be that we don't like what we see or that we just don't recognize at all who that person is looking back at us.

We find ourselves asking:

"How did I get here?"
  "What have I become?"
  "How did I let this happen?"

"Why did I not see this before now?"

At first, we may only make small changes in the ways we interact with and respond to others; for example a minor shift in the way we speak, act, or behave. We try convincing ourselves that one little compromise in what we know to be correct won't hurt.

"It's okay, it is just a little offense—no harm."

Then we do it again and again and again.

> **When you are doing something you are not supposed to do and are where you are not supposed to be, you are becoming somone you are not supposed to become.**

Over time, these little compromises begin to add up, changing the way we know to be our true selves. Perhaps it is in caring a little less about the people we work for or with or who work for us. Or maybe it is the type of parent, sibling, or friend we become. We wake up from this state of unconscious sleep with an awareness that we have become angry, mean, uncaring, selfish, and possibly even capable of causing harm to the very people we initially set out to help or those we care about most.

But why? For that promotion; to acquire a particular

material possession; for significance; for validation to compensate for some past hurt or insecurity? The reasons may be many, but the result is we are someplace we should not be, doing something we have no business doing, and have become someone who is not our true self.

When we are not ourselves and seek out our doctors, it usually results in getting a prescription of some type, whether an instruction we need to adhere to or one that we need to get filled at the pharmacy. In either case, the goal is to try to restore things back to par.

When we become aware of being out of place, we have the option of writing the prescription ourselves by deciding *This is not for me, not worth it, not who I am.* Deciding that something must change—starting with ourselves. No matter how hard, how painful, how impossible it may seem, we must trust that the present road will not lead us to where we want to go and that we will need to change course.

DISCOMFORT

When discomfort lingers beyond the initial phase, it usually occurs when we try to make what was not intended to be a resting place our home. Discomfort beyond the initial jolt can be a signal that we are persisting in a state for longer than we should be. In other words, we were not meant to stay in a place of the sting of pain and agony. We have work to do, things to accomplish, that exist beyond where we were just a few minutes ago.

Experience it. Move on. Get past it.

PAIN

In medical terms, pain is traditionally defined as being associated with an injury, either internal or external. The cause is typically related to the introduction of something foreign to the body; or, if the injury is internal to the body, is understood as some type of abnormally. In other words, something in the body is doing something or behaving in a manner other than the way it should.

We know from experience that during a crisis, we can experience pain in the absence of physical injury. For this to occur, the brain has to tell the body to hurt. Humans can experience many different types of pain. We can feel the stinging pain of loss in its various permutations. We can feel the stab of betrayal and broken trust. We can feel the gut punch of a personal attack—whether invited or not. In some cases it may feel like someone has ripped our heart out of our chest and stomped on it. The degree of pain we feel corresponds to our tolerance of pain. To whatever extent, however, we all experience it during the crisis, in one form or another; it is inevitable. How debilitating the pain is and how long it lasts, however, is dependent on us.

A betrayal might cause Sara to become upset to the point where she cannot function, while the same situation might be of no concern to Jack. Being embarrassed in public might be something that would send Jack into immobilizing fear paralysis, while Sara would remain unfazed facing the same situation.

Our capacity to endure pain and deal with the crisis, our capability to handle adversity, is dependent upon our coping ability. We are all unique beings who have experienced different environments. While the experiences might not always differ, our uniqueness as people combined with those experiences help to determine our coping ability and stress capacity.

PRESENCE
Our most potent, passionate presence comes from our deepest point of pain.

Things get real when we are in pain—especially when we

want strongly not to be in pain. My desire for my knee not to hurt was equal to my desire to not have to tell my dad I had totaled my car. Honestly, the thought of having to tell him felt more painful than my injuries.

Pain has a way of drawing and commanding our full and undivided attention. Little else matters in the moment when you slam your big toe into the sturdy leg of the couch that wasn't there yesterday. For a few seconds, the world seems to stop as all focus and attention is focused on the tremor shooting up and down your leg, pulsating from the point of contact throughout what feels like your whole body. We will stop at nothing to make the pain subside and go away at that moment.

> **When the pain of the present becomes greater than the fear of the future, that is when real growth begins to take place.**

The same holds true for peak crisis moments.

"What can I do to make this stop right now?"
    "What can I get rid of?"
    "Where can I move/go?"

Seldom are we more present than in that very moment. We feel stronger than ever about making a change. At the pinnacle of pain in the crisis, we are willing to do anything just make it stop.

When the pain of the present outweighs and becomes greater than our fear of the future, that is where and when real change begins to take place. It is at that moment we gain the courage to begin to change.

So we start to compare. This thing that I am doing, that I am holding on to, that is burning me, that is hurting me and causing so much pain; what will happen if I let it go? What will I lose?

One great example of this is a job you detest. We might hate what we do to earn a living, feeling like we are standing in place and doing the same thing day in and day out, feeling unappreciated and in some cases even mistreated. We still get up and go each day because we fear the pain of not being able to pay our bills, of not having a roof over our heads and food to eat. We believe that would be greater than the pain of our current, unfulfilling life.

And perhaps in some cases that may be true, in the short term. But for how long? I have experienced this myself. When we are at the sunset of our lives looking back, will we regret the time wasted being unfulfilled, doing something that we knew we shouldn't be out of fear—of what? Will our worst fears even materialize?

When we reach that point where we say to ourselves, "Even my worst fear—fear of being alone, of being broke, of losing my car or even my home—is better than continuing to endure the present situation," then is when we begin to make progress.

Don't get me wrong, this is not a suggestion to up and quit a job, relationship, or educational pursuit. We need to give thought to and have a plan to make changes that are favorable.

The major point here is this: when we are willing to let go

of things we are holding on to mainly out of fear, it opens up a vast span of opportunity that we might not otherwise have seen. In other words, if we are willing to risk letting go of what might be holding us back, we position ourselves to be able to advance and gain something much better. In short, it means living a better life, a fulfilling life, instead of merely existing in a mediocre or miserable one.

It can be a good thing when the pain of our present circumstances helps us break our grip on something we need to let go of in order to grow. We may have been unwilling because our security was attached to what we were holding on to. Sometimes it's a false idea, thought, or belief. Other times it's a material possession. In either case, our attachment to that thing, our fear of losing it even though it may not be right for us, is what is binding us to be stagnant, and we need to let go to be free.

Fighting and Resisting

It is better to be for something rather than against it. Fighting or resisting something we cannot change is a futile effort. Does that mean we should not battle? Not necessarily. Battle positions can be offensive or defensive. You have probably heard the phrase, "The best offense is a strong defense." Sometimes being prepared to fight means protecting something, while in other cases it means preventing it.

To be prepared for war is one of the most effective means of preserving peace. —George Washington

We can "battle" in our minds concerning the things we do control—our thoughts, and taking the offensive measure to prevent them from controlling us. The battles we wage, the wars we fight, are much more about the battleground that is internal than it is about things external.

For matters we do not control but can influence, it is better that we focus on what we can do, versus trying to control what we cannot. Mother Teresa once said, "I was once asked why I don't participate in anti-war demonstrations. I said that I will never do that, but as soon as you have a pro-peace rally, I'll be there."

When we are for something, our focus is on a solution, on what we want, as opposed to being against something, which means we are focusing on what we don't want, and in turn, getting more of it. Suffice it to say you will not get what you want by focusing on what you don't want.

DENIAL

You may have heard the play on words "Denial is a river in Egypt," referring, of course, to the River Nile. Apart from that use, the word serves little purpose in our lives—living in denial, that is. We can spend all the time in the world rejecting, justifying, compensating, bargaining, or telling ourselves mistruths, but the fact remains, that is time wasted. The trade-off for the perceived temporary escape from discomfort is just a delaying of the inevitable—the truth that we must face to move on.

> **Avoiding percieved pain will not prevent it, but instead create a perpetual purgatory.**

SELF-DISTRACTION

When you hear a noise indicating something is wrong with

your car, you don't turn up the radio to drown out the sound, do you? I liken this to making ourselves busy with fruitless activity. Only making more noise doesn't resolve the issue. In fact, it can make a small thing worse. Best to stop, be still, check it out, and then give thought to creating a plan of attack or a way to address the problem. Sometimes we need to be still, be in the present moment, and process rather than running to-and-fro with nonproductive, distracting activity.

WARPED PERSPECTIVE

Habitual resisting and denial can lead to a warped perspective. It can deeply influence our focus.

Focus, what we look at, expect, and concentrate on, is what steers and guides what we want, or don't want, directly to us. Our intensity in this area can lead to us imprisoning ourselves based on our expectations of how things should go or be. Inevitably, this can lead to disappointment, and even bitterness, when things don't go as we had imagined. Our span of control extends no further than ourselves, which is difficult enough to manage. Why then would we think we can control others, circumstances, or even nature?

> **You will not get
> what you want
> by focusing on
> what you don't want.**

W.Y.S.I.W.Y.G.

The tech world uses the acronym WYSIWYG. It stands for:

What
  You
  See
  Is
  What
  You
  Get

While initially this acronym was derived to describe computer user interfaces, it is also applicable for how our minds work. Often, what we look for and see becomes our experience—that works both ways, good and bad.

If we are always assuming the worst, looking for the worst, it should come as no surprise that most if not all of what we see is the worst outcome. From experience, I believe that this focus acts as a magnet attracting the things we obsess over.

We can, however, leverage our focus to work in our favor by choosing to concentrate on the positive aspects of what we can draw out of every situation. It could even be a negative situation, like a car accident, a broken limb, or a job loss. We can look for the good, the lesson to help us, the reason to be thankful in every circumstance. Looking first (and preferably only) for this, we stand to gain valuable insight that will help point us in the direction of a solution. This mindset helps shift us away from being stuck and engrossed in the problem.

The positive focus will also aid us in obtaining much-needed energy, inspiration, and mental stamina that will help combat fatigue and mental obstacles we face during a crisis.

WYSIWYG IN ACTION

I recall one humid afternoon in Florida (like there is any other kind) when my wife and I were enjoying a round of golf. The slight cloud cover would make the sunset come sooner than we had hoped; however, with a sparsely populated course, we played at our leisure.

Given my less-than-admirable golf skills, I believed the more strokes you made, the better value you received for your money. We pulled up to a short par-three hole that was about as straightforward and easy as they come. It had a few trees on each side. The right front of the green had a small sand trap that looked more like a gash from the removal of a tree stump than a hazard.

Since I tended to swing too hard, I picked my trusty five iron when a pitching wedge would have been more than enough for this short hole. I had hoped by choosing a longer club, I wouldn't swing as hard. I took a very smooth swing, connecting with the sweet spot, and watched the ball fly upward toward the hole until it was no longer visible.

Since I was satisfied my ball had landed somewhere within a stroke (or two) of the green, my wife hit, and we headed on our long journey to the green. We found her ball just on the edge but could not locate mine.

After a quick scan of the green, thinking it probably hadn't landed there, we began to search every area surrounding the green. Still no luck. From there I ventured well past the green into the fairway of the holes behind and to each side. Luckily there were no players behind us, so we had plenty of time to conduct this search and rescue—golf balls are not cheap.

I started to grow frustrated. I knew I hadn't hit *that* bad of a shot. My disposition began to shift from relaxed to borderline anger. My wife, sensing my mood change, decided to encourage or perhaps humor me and check the green again, including one part we hadn't—the cup. Lo and behold there, was my ball, in the hole— I'd hit my first and only hole-in-one.

So apart from the health benefits of the extra steps taken to search for my "lost" ball, how much time, focus, and energy did we waste unnecessarily? I hadn't even considered looking in the hole. Assuming the worst, things spiraled downward and turned an otherwise pleasant putting event and peaceful moment into a mini-crisis. All from failing even to consider the best-case scenario and automatically assuming the worst.

Even in the face of something like my subpar golfing skills, it is possible for something good to happen, for there to be a reason for optimism. Don't miss the great moments in life by being so busy searching for the worst.

Fortunately, there was a pro on staff that day to sign my card and, well, let's just say I live that moment over and over on PGA.com.

Hopelessness

Horror movies, sci-fi fantasies, action-packed, and drama-filled thrillers exist because of the creative human mind. Ideal for generating box office revenues . . . not so great when the mind is left alone to its own devices. Especially when it's allowed to conjure up the worst and most unfathomable scenarios and present them as potential truths.

Our thought life can affect our emotional state in such a way that it can cause us to lose all hope. It can drain us of energy and even cause us to lose the will to live. More on that later.

The truth of the matter is, however, that these catastrophic creations in our minds are thoughts—just that. In most cases they can't become real unless we do something to change them from thoughts to actions. We influence bringing them into existence through our actions as they seldom occur on their own. You should consider your thoughts as seeds. Some seeds you don't want to plant or water. There are others you need to dig up and dispose of never to be planted in the garden of your mind again.

**Your thoughts
will eat you alive
if you feed them.**

NO LONGER IMPORTANT

Hopelessness can leave you feeling like nothing seems important. It can draw you in with statements like:

"What's the point?"
  "Why even bother, it's just going to turn out bad again."
  "This is pointless."
  "That'll never work."
  "I'll never [fill in the blank]."
  "Who cares anyway?"

That mindset is the entry point into the danger zone. Think about hopeless thoughts as carbon monoxide: it lulls you to sleep before it kills you, so it is crucial that you *wake up*!

SELF-DOUBT AND SELF-LOATHING

This is pointless, so why should I bother? is a point of view that's a cousin to self-doubt and self-loathing. We can quickly spin out of control by beginning to question:

"What is so special about me?"
  "This has already been done anyhow."
  "Why should I bother, I don't deserve it."
  "I don't have anything special or unique."

"No one wants to hear, read, see what I have to offer."

"No one cares about me."

"I'm too bad of a person to matter because I [fill in the blank]."

"I've done too many wrong things to be of any help to anyone."

"Who am I to think I can help someone else?"

All of these are lies our minds repeat like a broken record, desperately trying to distract us, diminish our value, detract from our purpose, and prevent us from achieving our goals because we are too busy being distraught.

WHAT IF **MONSTER**

During bouts of hopelessness, I've certainly done my share of battle with the *What If* Monster.

"What if I lose my job / get laid off?"

"What if we lose our house?"

"What if we get evicted?"

"What if we run out of food?"

"What if the car breaks down?"

"What if I can't make the payments and they repo the car?"

I could go on and on toying with the musings of the *What If* Monster. That road leads to a haunted cul-de-sac of fear, constant anxiety attacks, and depression. Our genius minds become Steven Spielberg-quality directors creating movies that play back in an endlessness loop like a nightmarish merry-go-round that won't stop—that is, until you get off.

Surrender

I remember a time when I was traveling to Atlanta. Despite the challenges I was facing at the time, I was looking forward to the trip. I was in the process of writing this book. While waiting in line, I was mulling over how I had faced so many challenges in my life, yet I was still going, trying, enduring. I hadn't given up. *That is worth something*, I told myself. *That is worth sharing.*

At the moment, the doubting-Thomas voice in my head seized the opportunity to strike, and antagonistically chimed in with a barrage of

"Why would anyone be interested in hearing what you have to say?"
"What do you know about challenges?"
"What makes you an expert?"
"What experience do you have?"

The voice of apprehension went on and on with the self-doubt attack.

I countered with a positive thought:

"Great, short line today. Just a few people ahead of me."

As I approached the TSA agent, preparing to hand him my documents, I shot back in my head:

Enough! I know what I've been through, and if sharing it can help just one person, then it's worth it. Be quiet!

I handed the stoic-looking TSA agent my credentials and watched him review them, as a teacher would grade a paper. Then he uttered in an everyday, dry tone that matched his blank expression:

"You've been fighting your whole life."

I laughed out loud as he handed back my documents; I was accustomed to people making puns or comments about my last name. As I began to proceed to the baggage-screening checkpoint, I noticed that he wasn't laughing. I even felt a little awkward.

As I replayed the moment, I realized it was not a question but a statement. A true statement to be exact. I thought, *How did he know?* I'd never seen him before in my life. He was not even one of the regulars. I wasn't downtrodden or long in the face. I was upbeat, glad to be headed out, and happy about the short line. I turned back to see if he was still there but didn't see him.

At the moment it struck me how profoundly true that statement was. From childhood, I have been battling, nearly every day of my life, but I have endured. I embraced this event as a turning point and not a coincidence. I used it to put firmly embrace the decision to continue with the idea of this book and sharing. I simply had to.

That struggle, my struggle, this battle was for a reason. It felt like he was a messenger sent to let me know I was on the right path, that purpose, my mission for fulfillment, was just around the corner, and that this was about to pay off in the way of having a meaningful impact. I only needed to stay the course.

I felt an indescribable sense of peace, a sense of purpose, after that encounter. It was confirmation that I was, in fact, a subject-matter expert on challenges, especially enduring them, and that what I had faced could serve a greater purpose.

LET GO OF THE PAST

There comes a time when we realize that we cannot change the past, only learn from it. Just like we cannot control the future but should plan for it. To add to our load, we find that trying to control the present is just as overwhelming as the other two.

Surrender means to cease resistance, to give up or hand over possession, to abandon. We reach this place because we have come to the end, are just plain tired, or have tried everything we know to do to no avail. In any case, we are ready just to let go.

This not a surrendering or giving up on our dreams, hopes, or ambitions. We are waiving the white flag in acknowledgment of our lack of possession of control over what we now accept that we cannot, and never could, restrain.

We vow to stop fretting over what was or was not, what happened or did not occur. We stop living in fear of the future, what might happen, and focus on living in the present moment, what is, rather than what was.

ACCEPTANCE

Part of surrendering is to accept where you are in this current place. While where you are right now may not be or align with where you want to be in your future, it may be the path to your future. This premise is why we must realize and embrace how important it is to be present in the moment.

You may need to be on this very path, at this very place, at this very time, to get to where you're going. Part of letting go is accepting this moment and embracing it for what it is.

> **Where you are now**
> **may not be where**
> **you want to be,**
> **but may lead you**
> **to where you want to be.**

BREATHE

At this stage, we are most likely exhausted, spent, running on fumes. Endurance is not an endless race but rather a power that we leverage strategically to manage the crisis. As with any power, it needs to be renewed from time to time to remain potent.

In the heat of the moment, we tend to forget to breathe. Now that we have arrived at this place, we have let go; this is time to recharge, making a conscious effort to relax for a moment, to consciously breathe; letting go with each exhale and being grateful with each inhale.

At first, this phase requires conscious practice—Let Go, Relax, Breathe, repeat—until it becomes second nature again. You are refueling, recharging, preparing to break free from the endless cycle.

We will cover those phases more in-depth in the next chapters. For now, just *breathe*.

DON'T JUDGE

Don't be quick to judge—better not to at all. There is that

saying, "We are our own worst critics." During the crisis, we sometimes have the irresistible urge to first judge ourselves harshly, then others, and then ourselves again. We compare ourselves to others and then to the version of ourselves that we created in our minds that is mostly unrealistic.

To judge means one decides the results, is qualified to give an opinion, or has authority over. By that definition it is evident we have no business judging others, let alone judging ourselves. We can be aware of our behavior, how it affects others, and, in turn, how it affects us. We can then work to be a better version of ourselves, stopping, however, short of judging. That is not our place.

We do not control the outcome; we influence it, not by our opinions, but by our actions. It is challenging to be impartial even in the most optimal of conditions. If we are not good judges in general, it is fair to say we stink at it during a crisis. That's not a judgment, just a statement of fact.

POWER OF WORDS

Words are powerful tools. They can also be devastating weapons. Once uttered, they seldom can be taken back. This concept is also true for the self-talk that we allow to swirl around in our heads, whether directed at someone or something else or at ourselves.

Unconsciously, those words can lift us or level us without us even knowing it. We can sabotage our efforts without uttering a single word but merely by only the words in our thoughts.

Give up using or thinking words that don't serve a meaningful purpose. If you need to let out aggression, perform a physical activity like a walk, stomp, or run—you know, exercise. Clean, sort, dust. Move a box or four. Fix something. My point is, direct that energy toward something constructive rather than destructive.

Words can lift or level.
Are you growing
or grounding
with your speech?

Phases of Endurance in Crisis

In the next three sections, we are going to uncover the three phases of endurance in crisis. Simply put, they are:

- *Let Go*
- *Live Now*
- *Win*

Each of the phases addresses elements of the stages of endurance covered earlier in this book and how to manage and cope during a crisis. The end goal is to achieve peace in the midst of adversity.

This is the receipe for how you can become somone who never quits and learn to give everything you have to give.

Let Go

The first step in the three phases is to *Let Go*. Let go of the how and live in the now. Yesterday ended last night. The combined wealth of both Bill Gates and Warren Buffett cannot buy five seconds of yesterday.

The act of letting go is not a loss but rather a gain. We gain freedom from bondage. Freedom from trying to control what we cannot. Freedom from the impossible and the suffocating pressure connected to that, which is an unnatural existence.

> **You will not get to where you want to go by focusing on where you dont want to be**

HOW THE BRAIN WORKS

Okay, to master this process, let's first look at how the brain works. No, I'm not about to get into a lengthy scientific discussion on neurons and synapse firing and the sort. If you want to go down that path and explore further, I suggest you read the book *Who Switched Off My Brain?* by Dr. Caroline Leaf.

In her book, Dr. Leaf breaks down the thought process into simple terms we can all grasp. Essentially, the brain forms a thought. As our brain processes the thought, we develop an emotion about the thought—good, bad, or otherwise. That emotion we assign to the thought then turns into and drives our action and behavior. All this stems from that original thought.

THE THOUGHT PROCESS

Often we attempt to address and change things in our behavior with limited success. Since this is difficult and seldom effective, we grow frustrated. A simple analogy is that it's hard to catch a train that has already left the station.

Trying to prevent the matter that has already shown up in our behavior (action) is a futile effort that is too late. Better to address the issue at the thought stage. The key to making a change—real, long-lasting change—is to take action by capturing the issue at the thought development stage, not long after it shows up as an undesired behavior. We must decide and consciously learn to stop developing and assigning an emotion to thoughts that are counterproductive for us.

We can train ourselves, our brains, to jettison thoughts that do not help us, as they occur and *before* we develop an emotion about them. Then, as we all know, dwell on them like, *foreverrrrrr* (insert voice of a teenager with attitude).

By the time those negative thought critters show up in our behavior, we are about as successful at getting rid of them as we would be trying to shoo away the parade of kitchen ants from the morsel of food they found on the counter during the night. Especially when we see the endless trail of ants leading back into the nest buried in a land far, far away.

SLAYING THE WHAT IF **MONSTER**

We have a tendency to waste a lot of time worrying about what isn't. What if = what isn't.

Falling prey to this monster can come in the way of thought bombardment stemming from an overactive imagination.

In dealing a fatal blow to the *What If* Monster we spoke of earlier in the book, I had to learn to stand up and yell, with all the defiance of a spoiled, unchastened three-year-old:

"WHAT IF? So!! What if?"

Let's play this scenario out, bring it! Allow the mind to play out the whole torturous scene, step by step. But at each step, demandingly ask:

"And then?!"

Next horrific scene plays.

"And then?!"

The next.

"And then?!"

Let it unfold back and forth until the show has fully played out. Interestingly enough with this approach, the mind, being bullied back, begins to lose its confidence as it sees it is no longer tormenting you.

Let logic ensue. Ask, *what* if . . . I mean really, what *if*?! Imagine, envision, even feel—with a purpose. Be in control of this mind movie, driving through each scene—don't let it be thrown at or forced on you. There is a freeing power in playing it out forcefully, carrying in your back pocket the trump card yet to be put down:

"Okay, after all is said and done, we will pick up the pieces and start over".

Now, what?

This strategy renders powerless the oppressive mental sham. The power is in your expressed willingness to accept whatever happens coupled with a vow to continue after. The anxiety was fueled by the unknown. By envisioning it out of rebellion, you've disarmed the principal weapon used against you and turned it toward the attacker.

REALITY

With the onslaught of "reality" television shows in recent years, the term has gotten a bit, shall we say, overused. The intent of the literal definition is how things are as they exist, rather than our notion of them. It has been said that perception is reality in the mind of the perceiver. That, however, does not grant one license to mistake facts for mentally manufactured fiction.

So is how we perceive reality actual reality or just our perception? While reality is said to be something that is seen, the same holds true for perception, with one distinct difference. Perception involves and includes our understanding or interpretation as processed through our mental impression. This includes relying on our intuition and insight while also involving our nervous system and memory to help interpret.

What that means is while we may see, hear, and feel something in its actual existence, we can also warp and distort it during our mental processing. In other words, we have the ability to create realities that do not exist from those that actually do.

This happens much in the same way, whether we want to

admit it or not, when "reality" TV personalities are coached to create more drama; one can only get so worked up over cake after all. Our minds will create the same non-existent drama, working things up into such a frenzy that the unrealistic becomes realistic, that is until it meets reality head-on.

How many times were we convinced that a situation or someone's behavior was due to a specific reason or cause only to find out that what we thought was the farthest thing from the truth. Awkward; check, please. Reality check.

Learn to let go of a reality that does not serve you or disrupts your peace of mind. If it is an actual reality, there may be little you can do about it. If conceived and alive only in the small village of your mind, best that it remains there and be allowed to dissipate intentionally.

In either case, it is not worth the investment in time, energy, and emotion to get distracted or sidetracked by an overactive, creative mind. Write a script and send it to Hollywood if you must, but for your sake, don't live it out for free!

WORRY IS A WASTE

Many are the quotes about worry are from great philosophers, including Lao Tzu. They can be summed up this way: worry is focus on the future, and regret is focus on the past. Both are a waste of time; learn to focus on the here, the now.

I spent the majority of my life worrying about tomorrow while not living in the day. In every case, tomorrow always came. Of the thousands of days not once did it happen in the exact way I had envisioned in my worry. In those instances where I did experience what I was worried about, not once did the event consume my entire day.

While the situation may have been for a moment or period

during the day, there was still ample opportunity during that same day to experience life other than the strife. It was not ever as bad as I imagined it to be. In some cases, I was at peace that the struggle had peaked and had reached its conclusion.

What sense does it make to worry about tomorrow instead of living today, in the moment?

How do you eat Godzilla?

For you planners and detail-obsessed readers, let's assume he is free range, non-antibiotic, organic, vegan, gluten free, soy free, raw, non-GMO, fat free, low carb, and prepared rotisserie style or with teriyaki BBQ sauce or blackened, and served with rice, salad, noodles, in a sushi roll, or however you prefer him.

My point is that you would still eat him one bite at a time. Because attempting to consume Godzilla all at once would be overwhelming. You would choke, suffocate, and perhaps even die.

The same applies to living each day. We were designed to live moment by moment. Attempting to live today, tomorrow, next week, and next year all at the same time is no more practical than it is feasible. What we end up with is a debilitating, paralyzing, ineffectual existence, and we are torn between the natural and unnatural, rendered inoperative, and incapable of positive advancement and progression.

The word consume means to ingest, put away, or dispose of. How can we do that with something that does not even exist yet? Attempting to do so in our thoughts is both abnormal and irrational and also explains our harried, confused, dysfunctional, distrusted, non-peaceful state when we try.

For example, it took me years longer to write this book because I attempted to write it all at the same time. I don't mean in one sitting but rather the forward, table of contents, each chapter, and end matter all at the same time, instead of focusing on writing one word, sentence, a paragraph at a time.

BASIS OF OUR WORTH

How often do we self-assess? And during that assessment, how often do we factor in other's opinions of ourselves? While it's prudent to look for the nugget of truth in the feedback we receive from others we trust, we should also be careful.

First, we should extend trust only to those who have our best interest in mind. Preferably, those who have nothing to gain or lose by giving us feedback—they only want to help.

Then there are those who have ulterior motives. Too often their assessments are cloaked with self-preservation. These individuals lack self-confidence. Because of this, they seek to decrease your value in their minds so as to raise their own.

We should not base our worth or value solely on the assessment of others. The possibility is more likely if you are of or have high value—meaning you are focused on having a positive impact on others.

AFTER YOU'VE DONE ALL YOU CAN

There comes a time where you have done all that you can humanly possibly do. Any further effort will have a diminishing return and lead only to further frustration and probably upset.

At these times, it is okay to let go. Stop looking to escape. Instead, just experience the situation—it will soon pass. In other words, let it be, let it play out like a storm passing through. Once it has passed, assess the damage and move forward.

"The earth is round and the place which may seem like the
end may also be the beginning"
—*Ivy Baker Priest*

REJECTION

At times we inevitably feel rejected. These feelings can lead
to a sense of dejection. Thoughts of little self-worth, low self-
esteem, and devaluing ourselves can occur. It can start with
you asking yourself questions like:

"What's wrong with me?"
   "Why doesn't this person like me?"
   "What did I do wrong now?"

Which can then lead down a thought path of

"I'm no good."
   "I'm just a screw-up."
   "I always mess things up."
   "Nothing good ever happens for me."
   "I'll never succeed."
   "I'm a failure."

These are dangerous thoughts to allow to roam freely in our
heads. If we leave them unchecked, we run the risk of letting
them repeat so often that we begin to believe them. Over
time, the repetition can make them a reality. It is crucial to
swat down these types of toxic thoughts like a seven-foot-tall
center does when his opponent attempts to make a basketball
shot. To prevent toxic thoughts from defeating you, reject and
eject them!

> **To prevent a toxic thought from defeating you, reject and then eject it!**

COMMIT TO DETACH

Endurance requires making the commitment to detach, let go, and become separated from our expectations. Once we free ourselves from that, we can move about with agility and ease that is unencumbered by apprehension. We are free to be creative rather than being paralyzed in fear by our attachment to a set outcome.

It begins with baby steps, one moment and victory at a time.

RESISTANCE IS FUTILE

It is futile to resist what already exists, and even worse, that which is contrived only in our minds, as if somehow, that will make it all magically disappear. When we stub a toe, what's done is done. It will not help us to resist the pain. Let it flow. The same holds true with a crisis that exists or has already occurred.

The energy and focus spent on resisting is wasted effort and only further consumes our attention. By the very act of putting forth the effort, energy, and focus, we create more of what we don't want.

Don't try to resist or fight. Only experience it, and it will soon pass. You need your energy for more important efforts.

PUT IT IN THE CLOUD

In today's modern age of technology, we can now capture and store things "in the cloud." This capability frees up valuable storage space on our phones, tablets, and computers. It ensures we don't have to lug everything around with us but can access what we need when we need it.

The same concept can apply to our lives. In the letting go process, there is great value in writing it down (storing) and letting it go; the cloud in this instance being a journal.

If feeling wronged, write it down and let it go. If upset over something, write it down. Express your emotion, and then let it go and forget about it. Don't obsess and linger over it.

This approach is freeing. It lightens our load and frees up the brain to focus on what actually matters: solutions. It also helps prevent replaying the event over and over in our head as our brain struggles to remember it, causing further anxiety created by feeling like we need to remember everything. Write it down, let it go, put it in the cloud.

ENDURANCE

Endurance is more about letting go than grabbing hold. I am reminded of the story of the professor holding a glass of water and asking her students what it was. The usual responses were, of course, a glass half full or a glass half empty. But that wasn't the lesson.

The professor went on to say holding the half glass of water for a minute was not a challenge. However, if she continued to hold the glass with water in it for an hour or two or several, she would begin to experience fatigue in her arm, followed by pain, then numbness, and eventually her arm would give out. It was not the weight of the water in small quantity that would cause her arm to give out, but rather the extended amount of time she held on to it.

The ability to endure has as much to do with letting go of what does not serve us any longer as it does actively carrying the current load of what we need to address right now.

UNBEARABLE MANAGEMENT

There are times when trying to manage the unbearable can feel completely overwhelming. At times it is as though our thoughts are flying at us at warp speed. We experience anxiety-inducing attacks that feel like they are swirling around us completely, engulfing us, trying to suffocate us.

It is at that very moment we must stop and ask:

"What are they doing to me right now?"
   "How is this hurting me right now?"
   "What impact does this have on me right now?"
   "Is this harming me right now?"

This approach is called *managing the moment*. We will often find that there is no imminent threat, but instead we are focused on our concern over something that may or may not occur in the future. Once we come to that realization, we reduce the tension down to a manageable level by reminding ourselves that "there" is not here yet and we will deal with "there" when and if it happens.

Use this effective strategy to manage your current load whenever it becomes overwhelming.

WHACK-A-MOLE

Thoughts that repeatedly pop up, and our subsequent need to deal with them, is very much like playing the whack-a-mole game. While it can be frustrating, if at the same you get into a rhythm and flow (or zone) of whacking them, it can be very gratifying.

Yes, occasionally one will slip by, and you may miss a thought here or there. But the important part is that you develop the habit of crushing the thought moles by knocking them down as your initial reaction to them appearing.

With practice, you eventually get to the point where you can do it instinctively. In life, that's called your subconscious. Striking down those opposing thoughts without even thinking about it is mastery of the whack-a-thought (mole) game.

THE FALLACY OF THE FACADE

We know that some houses have large, ornate or stately entrances designed to increase curb appeal. Those structures appearing to be solid brick, marble, or granite columns are in fact facades of the real thing. They're built to give the appearance of substance, but behind the disguise of a sturdy exterior lies a shallow or hollow core.

We can extract a lesson from this about our lives. Being honest with ourselves, we can look at what role personal pride plays in our lives. Are we trying to project an image of ourselves that is a facade to seek to impress others? If so, why? Does this increase when we are in the midst of a crisis as we try to cover up our human frailty, lest we risk exposing ourselves as vulnerable (also know as human)?

Yes, sadly, our society is overwrought with this internal illness of one-upmanship. We have become slaves to keeping up with the Joneses, and we react to what *Everybody* will think. I for one have chosen to move out of the neighborhood where the *Joneses* live, along with their relatives, the *Everybody* and the *They* families.

We unnecessarily place a heavy burden on ourselves that doesn't pay our bills or help us raise our families and certainly doesn't germinate into long-lasting, genuine friendships or relationships.

Nowhere is this more apparent than in the heart of the crisis. When you are dealing with an already unbearable challenge, the added load of trying to keep up a false image can sap what little remaining energy you have left to fight with. At the exact wrong time and place (when else does it occur?) it can even cause you to snap.

Learn to manage proactively, and prevent this breaking point by saying, "To heck with it! This is who I am, take it or leave it. If you cannot accept me for who I am and for my life's challenges that I am working through, then I most likely cannot depend on you to help me with them. You will probably end up making things worse, so you may go, leave."

If you are required to put up a facade to be someone you are not to maintain a relationship, that is not a relationship you need as it has no value. It is not one that is based on a foundation of authenticity and trust but rather sits on a thin sheet of translucent tissue paper ready to rip apart at the slightest stressor.

There is a Japanese teaching called *wabi-sabi* that puts this into perfect perspective. The philosophy of instruction is based on the premise of acceptance of imperfection. In his book *Wabi Sabi Simple*, Richard Powell describes *wabi-sabi* as "nothing lasts, nothing is finished, and nothing is perfect."

Choosing not to put effort toward maintaining the fallacy of perfection will help you store up much-needed energy reserves for where and when they are needed, rather than wasting them on impressions that just don't matter.

LET GO AND EMBRACE THE NOW

Upon hearing the diagnosis that I had cancer, the first thought that entered my mind was,

Oh my God, I'm going to die! OH My God, I'm going to die! I AM GOING TO DIE!

That is until I came to the realization that there was nothing new about that statement. Eventually, we are all going to die. Every single one of us has an expiration date—we just don't know what it is.

In the days after receiving my diagnosis, enduring a battery of tests checking to see if and how far it had spread, I engaged in significant battle with the *What If* Monster. I only found solace when I reached the point where I accepted reality. *I have cancer, and there is absolutely nothing I can do to change that fact—nothing. There isn't a thing that can undo it or prevent it at this point. It exists whether I like or agree with it or not.*

The old me who existed the day before was gone. Life as I knew it was gone—forever. It wasn't until I embraced that fact and said to myself, *Okay, now what are you going to do about it?* did I began to heal and resume forward momentum.

During the discovery process before treatment, the time of uncertainty, I learned to embrace my new life by seeking and finding the positive, the hope, the happiness and, yes, the joy wherever I could find it. I became more thankful for the years and experiences I had enjoyed and people I had shared them with to that point in my life. I became more grateful for the moments and days. I let go of what I had no control over and accepted and embraced my new life. I resolved to live each day, each moment, regardless of the eventual outcome.

EXPECTATION PRISON

How many times have we had or set an expectation for something and it did not turn out as we had hoped? We then became upset because our expectation hadn't been met. Over repeated instances of this, we can grow increasingly frustrated and eventually bitter. We become rigid and confined in our way of thinking how things should be, how people should act, and the outcome that should take place.

We then find ourselves spiraling downward in a well of disappointment after disappointment until we feel trapped. What got us there? Our own expectations. I refer to this as *Expectation Prison*. It is a mental, not physical, cage we have confined ourselves to.

We are detained and growing increasingly upset at the loss of our freedom to enjoy life by this false cell we have created in our minds. The saddest part is that the door unlocks from the inside, and we are the only ones who hold the key.

That is also the good news. If we are willing to let go of our expectation on how things should be and simply accept them as they come and for what they are, we will enjoy an uninhibited freedom that will change our lives for the better. It is only a matter of deciding in our minds that we will no longer be held captive to the mental images we created of how the world should exist. We have no authorship or claim to creating, controlling, and ruling over any of it. We can only influence and control ourselves.

By letting go of our confining expectations, we award ourselves a pardon from a mental death row. This is a clemency that we can give ourselves anytime we chose—no questions asked. The only thing we are guilty of is putting ourselves in expectation prison in the first place.

**Divorce your past
and fall in love with,
marry, and live you now
into your future.**

Youicide

I recall vividly one of my lowest low points. I had replayed the past in my head so many times that it began to feel like the bad from yesterday was still occurring.

Suffice it to say that loop had an enormous impact on my hope for a better future—which at that point was nonexistent. Deep in despair and doubt over wondering if things would ever get better, I began to think thoughts like *You would be better off dead; you would be of more financial value to your family if you were dead instead of alive.* I had quite literally lost the will to live.

Trying to escape the suffocating feelings, I drove to the beach, one of my favorite places to just sit and think. Being near nature sometimes helps me get out of a funk. As I sat in my parked Jeep, looking at the endless waves flowing to the shoreline, receding, then repeating, I likened the never-ending cycle to that of my life: same thing day in and day out, week over week, month over month. I began to think, *I don't really care to go on anymore.*

The voice in my head continued:

What would it be like if you were no longer here?
Would people care?
Would they cry?
Would they miss you, and if so, for how long?

Why would they miss you?

You wouldn't have to deal with those problems that are bugging you anymore.

You wouldn't have to strive anymore to achieve that which has so far been unattainable.

You wouldn't have to feel the pain or disappointment over unmet expectations and let downs anymore.

You would leave enough money to take care of your family, so it'll be okay.

You wouldn't have to feel like a failure anymore.

No more feeling alone.

No more fighting.

As I sat contemplating what it would be like to no longer exist, I heard a loud bang.

It sounded as though the canvas top of my Jeep had been pierced. While it didn't startle me, it drew my attention as it had come from only a few feet away. As I looked around, I saw the guy in the car behind me jump out and run toward one of the benches that faced the natural beach grass area in front of the ocean.

I quickly followed in that direction, running across the strip of grass next to the sidewalk. In what seemed like a dream scene, with each step I took I went farther and farther into this surreal place.

I approached a woman who stood hysterically crying; she seemed to be in complete shock. As I moved past everything seemed to slow down, I observed the look of horror and fear in her eyes, which held a helpless expression of *Do something!* I then passed the guy from the car parked behind me, who was on his phone calling 911. I continued on as if being drawn to some place until I reached a gentleman on the ground, who to me looked like a Harold.

He lay sprawled across the grass in his recently pressed, untucked, long sleeve pink polo shirt and khaki shorts. Wondering if perhaps he had slipped off the bench, I looked up and saw blood splattered across the back of the seat next to where he had been sitting when I drove up and parked.

He was spread out awkwardly on the grass; one of his Sperry Top-Siders was partially on the sidewalk, the shoe's sole facing up. He was gasping for breath when he inhaled, in a stuttering manner followed by a long pause, and then an exhale. His strained breathing continued but with more extended periods between each unnatural sounding breath.

I drew in even closer, so close I could almost touch him. As I leaned over toward him, I realized that it was not just blood on the bench and green blades of grass.

Given the sizable hole on one side of his head and a small hole dripping blood on the other, it was apparent those were the entry and exit wounds caused by the large caliber gun barrel peering out from underneath his pink shirt; the weapon looked as if his body was protecting it.

It was evident there was nothing that any of us could do as we waited for the paramedics and police to arrive. I watched Harold struggle to take what appeared to be his last breaths. I wondered why had he chosen to do this to himself. I wanted so badly to ask him what was it that was so terrible, so wrong; that he thought this was the only way out.

The scene unfolded in a way that looked nothing like how the movies and TV portray suicide. It was not quick or clean. There was nothing about this that even remotely resembled what I had previously seen glamorized. It appeared that part of the brain remained and was still functioning, causing the body to struggle to breathe on its own, while the rest of him seemed to be lifeless.

I stood next to him, continuing to wonder, *How bad was it?* Why did he think this was the only option?

I listened to him struggle to breathe and for the next

one, he responded with another stuttered gasp for breath.

"Why did you do this?" I wanted to ask. "What brought you to this low of a place? Did you really feel there were no other options?"

[*stuttered gasp for breath*]

The color slowly faded from his pale legs, arms, and face, and the delay between stuttered gasps for breath grew longer. I looked up the sidewalk at the lady, still hysterical, who stood a few feet away from the guy from the car. By now a small crowd had formed from the people passing by on their evening stroll along the beach. All of them had the sense to maintain a safe distance.

Being so caught up in my morbid curiosity, I suddenly realized that I was standing over the body of someone who had a bullet in or go through his head. Even if it was self-inflicted, this was about to become a crime scene, and I was standing right in the middle of it. Common sense prevailed, and I walked over to where the others were standing just as the police and paramedics began to arrive.

Like clockwork, the yellow tape went up; the growing crowd was ushered back as the emergency vehicles reached the location. The scene then began to resemble what I'd seen on TV or movies as the officers asked if anyone knew or saw what had happened.

The few of us who were first on site offered to provide what little we knew. Because I'd parked right next to where this gentleman had chosen to take his life, my vehicle was inside of the yellow-tape area. I had plenty of time to reflect on what had just happened while I waited.

Howard eventually expired, a sheet was pulled over his body, and the crime scene investigators systematically went about the task of executing their various roles, as they had obviously done many times in the past.

Eventually, I was allowed to leave. I waved at the officer whose blank expression did not change as he lifted the yellow tape to let me drive away.

Later that night as I replayed the events in my mind, there was a jolt of reality in the surreal nature of what had felt more like a dream. How was it that I was sitting beachside contemplating having lost the will to live while someone else within feet of me felt the same way and decided to act on it?

Being so close to it and seeing it happen up close made it evident to me that this was not the "way out" or a solution to even consider, even before taking into account what he must have gone through physically. One thing was clear: suicide was *not* the answer.

Too frequently I have heard stories from co-workers and friends of their parents, relatives, friends, and loved ones who have committed or attempted suicide. In every case where it did happen, there was unspeakable devastation, and always, always, always the lingering, unanswered question of, "What could have been so bad that this was the answer?"

In every instance when someone attempted suicide but did not succeed, the response after the failed attempt was, "I don't know why I thought things were so bad that I felt like suicide would be the answer. Nothing was bad enough to make this the best choice." Each expressed thankfulness that it didn't happen, and were grateful to have a second chance.

A vivid example of this was the story a co-worker, Lori, shared with me. Lori's mother had once attempted suicide. Being a doctor herself, she knew the exact pills to take to stop her heart. Fortunately, she was discovered and rushed to the hospital before the pills took her life.

The following day, Lori's mom shared with her that she was very thankful her attempt at suicide had failed. She went on to say she didn't know what was so bad, so wrong that it was worth taking her own life. Lori's mom was grateful to have a second chance at life. Two days later, her mom's heart failed and she passed away. The cause stemmed from the attempted overdose.

As you might imagine, Lori was devastated. Not only had she lost her mother, with whom she was close, but it also came after it appeared things were heading back in the right direction. Fraught with despair and a myriad of overwhelming emotions, Lori faced a crossroads: become angry, bitter, and malcontent, or look for whatever good she could find in the situation. She chose the latter.

As a result, Lori has become resilient, learning to focus on living life, the things that matter, and letting that permeate throughout all of her interactions with others she meets. She knows firsthand that life is a gift and not infinite. Lori lives her life with a purpose, a resolve to experience all that it has to offer, and has an intense focus on trying to make the world better off for her having been here. She chose to live and enjoy life rather than allow her personal tragedy to consume and take that away from her too.

Committing suicide would mean the end of life as I knew it. Meaning all that was bothering me, all that was angering, frustrating, upsetting, overwhelming me would no longer matter. It would forever sever my connection to all of it. Life would still go on, just without me.

I began to listen closely to myself, to the voices in my head, to find out what I felt was so bad. Why had I lost the will to live, to go on? What was bothering me?

As I intently listened to myself, I heard:

> You *expected life to be different.*
> You *planned for things to happen in another way.*
> You *would like things a certain way.*
> You *expected people to act one way instead of another.*
> You *thought that if you did "x," everything would be okay/be better.*
> You *felt that something …*
> You *wanted …*
> You *believe that …*
> You *thought life should be different*

Then it dawned on me: suicide was most certainly not the answer, but that I needed to commit *YOUicide.* I did not need to end my physical life. That would be wrong. What I needed to do was separate myself—sever, disconnect, end—my connection with the YOU (I) had created in my head, just as if I were no longer here.

If I was willing to let go of my life (having lost the will to live), then most certainly I could be ready to let go of everything, and I do mean *everything*, as if I didn't exist, yet continue to live. I would accept whatever happened.

It was as if I had adopted the mindset of "If you knew you only had one day left to live, what would really matter?"

In many ways, this was a fresh start, even if it meant starting over; I was still alive. What a revelation! I felt completely rejuvenated! It was as though someone had lifted a massive weight off my shoulders. It was my second chance; I could wipe the slate clean and reboot. Mentally, I had no attachment to anything, so I no longer had to claim or attach myself to the crisis, nor to the pain and the suffering and overwhelming weight it brought. I was free —and more important, alive and excited to *live*.

I was able to cross this chasm by letting go of the mental attachment that weighed me down by accepting whatever might come and being willing to walk through it. The reward was the experience of a new beginning that felt like the difference between the crushing pain of lungs gasping for air in thick, black smoke and breathing in the refreshing, light, and crisp, clean air while walking along a picturesque shore in Hawaii. Best of all, I felt alive to actually to *live*, not just exist.

Live Now

Learn to live in the now, the present moment. In his book *The Power of Now*, Eckhart Tolle said it well when he explained that all we ever really have is now. He stated that the past is gone. I've heard it restated elsewhere as "Yesterday ended last night." He writes that "when the future comes, it comes as the now."

We must learn to live in the now, this present moment. Unfortunately, we have a tendency to live in the past. Recalling and reliving what did or did not happen in the past. In addition to doing that, we also attempt to live in the future. We stress ourselves out with what hasn't even happened yet by pre-living what might be.

It is like robbing ourselves of the now, the present moment, by living in the future or in the fear of and anxiety from worry over a past we cannot change.

When and then (the future and the past) are enemies of now—the present.

We must not spend our finite time trying to re-live or pre-live. We must spend it to *live*!

PROGRESS INHIBITORS

How many times have we used the word *when*?

"I will when . . ."

"When this or that occurs I will . . ."

"When I find time . . ."

"When the time is right . . ."

"When this event occurs . . ."

"When that happens . . ."

I call this the *after syndrome.*

"After this or that . . ."

"Will wait until after . . ."

"It will be easier then."

"I will get it done faster (false) quicker, easier then."

In some cases, perhaps in the short term, this might be possible, but be cautious of and careful not to allow that to be a reason to procrastinate.

Allowing the mind to embrace that it is okay to delay, put off, wait, or procrastinate is not advised. It will learn to create a comfortable reason why not to do something.

A LIFE ON HOLD

How often do we put something off until "when"?

"When I lose weight."

"When I get a new job."

"When the kids grow up."

"When I meet someone."

"When this series or season is over."

When! When! When! (Spoken like, *"Marsha! Marsha! Marsha!"* for those old enough to remember.)

Waiting until *when* is like throwing a party and inviting *when* but waiting to enjoy or experience the party until *when* arrives. Except, when *when* arrives, it shows up as *now*.

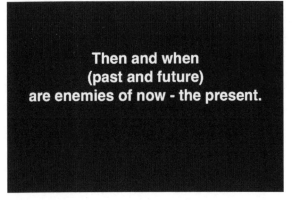

**Then and when
(past and future)
are enemies of now - the present.**

DANGER ZONES

Glasshouse dwellers—we've all seen and heard of them. They are the people with smudged windows; I'm talking dry, crusty, peanut-butter-and-jelly-half-circles-layered-on-top-of-each-other smudges.

They're the ones always in your ear telling you all the negatives about others and—of course—you. They are also the ones who send hate messages your way; they hate what you stand for, so they try to tear you down by implying you are not good enough, capable enough, strong enough, smart enough, good-looking enough, fill-in-the-blank enough.

They cannot bring themselves to stand up and put forth the effort to improve themselves for a better life—why, that just sounds like too much work. So instead, they put their time and energy toward tearing others down so they have company in their misery. It is an endless quest that is enjoyed only briefly for the few moments of despair they extricate from their latest victim.

To be clear, the people in your corner whom you can actually trust don't have anything to gain from you achieving your goal. They are genuinely happy for you and, quite frankly, know precisely how to tell you that you have bad breath without crushing your spirit. This is because they took the time to get to know you, are humble and secure in themselves, and can be happy for others who are making progress or succeeding in life. Anyone else who has critical feedback for you is suspect.

ISOLATION

Do not—I repeat, do *not*—try to do it alone.

Avoid isolation like the plague because it devours your energy, your faith, your hope, and spirit. Isolation differs from planned quiet or alone time that we all need to refresh.

Isolation leaves you completely vulnerable to the voices of the crazy family that lives in your head. These people are dysfunctional to an extreme, and while they may not be ill intentioned, they are just plain nuts.

The voices will say, imagine, and react to just about everything—the more insignificant, the better. They are the expert mountain-out-of-a-molehill makers. Too much time spent alone with our thoughts during the crisis puts us at risk of being severely affected. It zaps our energy, dashes our hopes, and possibly leads to a downward spiral of depression, anxiety, and hopelessness. We don't mean to despair; it's just how our mind works.

The good news is that a single conversation with the right person can vaporize the mountain of despair. It could be the very first time you've spoken with this person, or it may be someone with whom you have a well-establish relationship. They know just the right thing to say or not to say.

With the nest empty and my wife working hundreds of miles away, I've spent countless agonizing hours in isolation. Six days a week I wake up by myself, eat breakfast by myself, have dinner by myself, and go to bed alone.

As a result, I've experienced some of the deepest states of despair, engulfed in a thick cloud of hopelessness and suffocating unnecessarily. Fortunately, there were times when, having no clue what I was going through, someone reached out unexpectedly and helped pull me out. But not always, which is why it's not worth risking venturing down that dark alley alone. Have someone at both ends and others poking their heads out of doors along the way. You will be glad you did.

When things get tough, we have a tendency to become cave dwellers. This behavior is especially common for guys. We struggle with the feeling of not wanting anyone to know what we are facing, fearing that it will make things worse. Or we are plagued with the typical, stubborn "I'm tough and strong, and I can get through this on my own just fine."

That is until we find ourselves in a tight spot, halfway up the mountain, and then realize we left a bag of climbing supplies with the extra rope and carabiners back at camp. Then you think, "Wouldn't it be nice to have a climbing buddy toss you an extra clamp so you can rest for a minute?"

If facing or enduring a crisis, purposely plan to engage in human interaction with the right people. It doesn't have to be long and drawn out. It doesn't have to be a pity party—please don't do that. It may just be a quick phone call checking in on someone, or a cup of coffee or a milkshake.

Make it a point to have some form of interaction to remind you there is a whole other world outside of the one you are living in—the world that only exists in your head. This simple act can restore hope and invigorate and encourage you to stay the course. It can motivate you to hang in there, knowing that one day this will be behind you.

REST AND HEALING

In all of our enduring, we must not forget the importance of taking the time to rest and heal. A crisis usually calls for a burst of expending energy. We leverage the surge in adrenaline to manage the crisis. While useful in the moment, if we don't take the time to recharge, we run the risk of depleting our energy stores.

When we sustain an injury to our body, it takes time to heal. How much time partly depends on our body's ability to heal but also the severity of the injury. The same holds true for a crisis. The greater the crisis, the longer it may take to recover. Sure, we may think we feel and seem fine, but we might not have calibrated what is normal after an extended period of being on the high alert that stems from a crisis.

In a crisis, especially during the heat of it, it is crucial that we find or make time to rejuvenate. We must capitalize on the gifts of moments when there is even the slightest break in the action. It may be a few hours, a few days, a weekend, or even a week.

We make the mistake of thinking we need to stay "on" all the time, to be ready. Then we wonder why we get knocked flat on our backs by a blow that we withstood so easily before. It is because we are fatigued. Even the strongest of body builders experience fatigue. They have rest days—because of the severe crisis they put their muscles through trying to build them.

Meditation, yoga, a visit to the park or beach, or even a walk in an open field are powerful antidotes to mental fatigue. Find a place where you can go to escape mentally for rest. That may be in your bedroom, bathroom, or closet with your favorite relaxing music or earplugs!

A place where you can "stop the world" so to speak. Start by consciously focusing on breathing.

Inhale, 2, 3, 4 . . . exhale, 2, 3, 4.

The benefits are twofold. First, you're restoring healthy breathing and bringing precious oxygen into your body and secondly, by mentally focusing on breathing (say it out loud if it helps), you are not thinking about anything else at that moment.

Yes, it might seem unrealistic to neglect what requires your attention in the middle of a crisis. You can, however, always find or make time for a mini retreat to recharge, heal, and refresh. Every great soldier needs to recoup and re-energize, even in the heat of battle. Otherwise, you run the risk of exhaustion, breakdown, and even friendly fire—meaning you can sabotage yourself by fighting yourself.

WISHING VERSUS BELIEVING

Wishing is not the same thing as believing. Wishing is hoping for the possibility of something that may transpire. Believing is a resolute internal knowing as if it has already occurred, it already exists, and you are just focusing your view and sight on it while it comes into focus.

To simply wish for something does not bring it into existence. In support of the action we take, we must believe, know that it is possible. The impact of our determined belief instills confidence in our actions, further increasing the effectiveness of our efforts. Believing imparts a mental focus where we look for and expect what we are seeking, thus increasing our chances of realizing our goal.

WORK STRIFE

We've all been there: the boss from hell. Co-workers who act like wolves raised them. Working environments that are so caustic they feel suffocating. Maybe you are dealing with the stress of being overworked, feeling underpaid, or being under-appreciated.

The additional amount of pressure work stress can add to a crisis can be overwhelming. Most of us need to work to survive. For others, work provides a way of staying active. Because it's necessary, we give it a priority higher than almost everything else in our lives. That mindset then leads us sometimes to place too high of a priority on our careers.

I know this intimately from a missed opportunity. Since my wife and I work so far apart, we get to spend only a short amount of time together—about a day each week. Suffice it to say that any extra time is priceless.

My wife had taken a week off work so we could go on vacation to celebrate my being a one-year cancer survivor. At the time I was in the middle of a highly complex implementation of a new project at work. I felt that if I took time away, something might go wrong. I believed I could not step away right then—that work was too important.

I opted to keep working, leaving my wife alone to spend the time off by herself. We both needed a break after what we had been through over the course of the previous year. Vacation still occurred, only with one of us missing and the other all alone. I justified my decision by telling myself I was making a sacrifice for the company and my career.

By the time my second-year anniversary as a cancer survivor rolled around, things at work had significantly changed. While I could not have possibly imagined it at the time, due to a set of unspeakable circumstances, I no longer had anything to do with that project. As I sat and reflected, it felt like a punch to the gut.

What was so important? I thought, *What was worth passing up taking much-needed and deserved time off to spend with my wife?!*

As it turned out, all I had done was miss out on an opportunity that would never come again, and for what? I would have never predicted the outcome of that assignment and had sacrificed something far more valuable and important. I could never get that time or opportunity back.

I allowed myself to experience the pain and let it sink in. Then I let it dissipate. I only held on to the lesson I had learned. That lesson was: the future is never guaranteed, no matter how hard you work. Take each day, each moment, and live it. Celebrate the moments that deserve to be honored, and above all, never, ever put your job or career above things that matter more—like relationships and your own well-being. The cost is much higher than any reward.

FIRST STEP: YOU

To forgive someone, we must first forgive ourselves.

To love someone, we must first love ourselves. Too often we don't achieve our dreams, our visions, because we do not feel worthy. As part of the healing process, we must learn to forgive and love ourselves.

Start by accepting your imperfections. By our very nature we are flawed. We all make mistakes. Own yours. Forgive yourself. Embrace the consequences. Then extend compassion to yourself by loving the imperfect you. Spend less time judging yourself as compared to others and more time seeking to develop and grow into a better version of you.

FRIENDS, FANS, AND FOES

In our life's pursuits, if we are even remotely social, we have friends, fans, and foes. It is important to know the difference. Friends are those who have earned your trust and look out for you with nothing to gain personally.

Fans are those who are on your bandwagon, supporting your cause, so long as the benefit to them is greater than the cost. Expect them to abandon ship the moment they feel they need to invest more than they signed up for as it relates to commitment, effort, reputation, relationships, and, of course, money.

Foes are those who are dead set against what you stand for. Don't take this personally. In most cases, your purpose, mission in life, and passion pose a threat to them or their security. They may present themselves as fans or even friends, but make no mistake: it is only done to gain insight into how to make it easier to derail your effort. Always know the difference.

- Build your cause utilizing the cornerstones of friends.
- Market it and gain exposure for additional support through fans.
- Leverage your foes to energize your sense of purpose. Any great feat ventured for a good cause that will ultimately benefit others will undoubtedly have detractors. Having foes when you are attempting to make a positive difference is often a sign that you are on the right path. Let the existence of your foes encourage

you. Learn to recycle the bad energy they emit into fuel to help you along your way.

WHO'S IN YOUR CORNER

Engage and surround yourself with visionaries who get it, get you, and are supportive. They will help exterminate the mind imps trying to destroy you from the inside out! Visionaries feed us, propel us, and energize us.

These people act as cheerleaders, cheering you on even when it seems like the other team is wining. They may be close family members, co-workers, friends, classmates, a professor, a professional peer or even your barber or hairstylist.

You don't need an army. Just a few strong, intelligent, good hearted individuals who have nothing to gain by keeping your best interest in mind.

PHYSICAL PAIN AND MENTAL EUPHORIA

When you reach the place of extreme crisis it can be exceptionally taxing; you can feel like you don't have an ounce of energy left to expend. The caustic circumstance can physically drain you to the point of total exhaustion, and in some cases, writhing pain. This stage is a dreadful place to be.

Normally we are there both physically and mentally, which is the worst case. However, I have found that it is entirely possible to be there physically but *not* mentally. In fact, you can experience physical Armageddon while experiencing mental euphoria at the same time.

I've come to know this as being at the deepest point in the valley when you hit bottom and are about to cause the mental anguish to begin to propel upward. The key rests in knowing that you have reached the limit in your mind, and are becoming optimistic about the next chapter, season, course, or path on which you are about to embark.

The shift in focus occurs in part because you realize the situation cannot be worse than it already is, and in part because of the renewed strength and energy gained in the win of deciding that crisis may have worn you down physically, but you will not let it break you. When I reached this point, I adopted the phrase, "Battles don't break." You can use your own name or moniker; it is equally effective.

ON PURPOSE

Live your life on purpose, not by happenstance or accident.

"Well, if this happens, then I guess I will . . ."

"I might be interested in pursuing that if this other thing falls into place."

Live life with intent. Decide what you want and go after it. Don't be afraid of resistance or even failure. Find your passion, and make up your mind that you will strive to achieve it. Yes, you may have to change course along the way, but at least you are on your way to somewhere and taking strides to attain your goal.

Also, know that there is more to goal attainment than just speaking about it. While affirmations are an important part of achieving your dreams, living intentionally takes discipline and determination, not just declaration.

AUTHENTIC SELF

Above all, be your authentic self. Earlier we talked about being someone you are not and the fallacy of the facade.

If you find yourself struggling to be someone you are not, just stop. A crisis has a way of tempting us to take on a different persona or wear a different mask as we try to cover up the pain, embarrassment, or sadness. We end up building a fake life that does not reflect who we actually are. That is then added on top of the challenge we are already enduring.

When you are your authentic self, you don't always have to remember who you are trying to be and get into character. That's a very challenging act to maintain when our nerves are raw, the pain is peaked, and emotions are turbulent.

Further, we beat ourselves up after the fact for not being ourselves.

Let's not add fuel to the fire. Know who you are and be yourself. Those who leave were meant to—let them go.

Live as you, not as the version of you created in your head or the version the world tries to pass off as you. Live *your* authentic life.

SEARCHING IN THE WRONG PLACE

You may recall the song performed by Johnny Lee, "Looking for Love in All the Wrong Places." Searching for a solution in the wrong place is quite similar.

Like when we are always checking our email inbox or surfing online for an answer when the answer already exists inside of us. We may look in our mailbox or to other people, thinking they have the answer, but many times it has already been given to us. We may not like it or may choose to ignore it, but that doesn't change the fact that it exists within us, and not "out there."

The song goes on to talk about looking for love in different faces. Written more than twenty years before Facebook, FaceTime, and Face Swap, that second verse still offers relevant wisdom.

LISTEN, BELIEVE & KNOW

Pay attention to that seductive inner voice trying to tell you what you cannot do. Its intent is merely to distract you from focusing on your goal and pursuing your purpose. Skip wasting time trying to fight or resist it. Be aware of its sultry attempts to defeat you. Avoid falling into the trap of listening unconsciously and falling into embracing the message as the only truth.

Now, believe that what you know in your heart to be true can in fact become real. Know that despite what you may hear in the negative self-talk and may think based on what you hear, your dream, your goal, your aspirations can come to pass.

Believe and know that it will happen with an indomitable will that is not moved or dissuaded by what it may hear (and to associated faulty beliefs of defeat before action).

What should you do when faced with the inevitable pain and hardship of present suffering?

You believe.
You know.

Not waiting for a feeling, or acting in some ritualistic manner of rehearsed response but, rather, knowing. When every fiber of your being says it's possible, yet every outward indication screams "No way," you remain believing. Refuse to base your belief on what you see but rather what you know to be true, at your core.

This place is the place where you experience peace. The peace that is a calm, collected, reserved presence, irrespective of the turmoil that immediately surrounds you.

Know, believe, and persevere despite what you are facing. Funnel the pain, anxiety, and fear as fuel to strengthen rather than giving into its crushing, smothering, suffocating, stifling menagerie of the facade.

DON'T GO IT ALONE

We humans have a tendency to shut people out and retreat to our caves in times of crisis. Bad idea.

There are, of course, instances where we don't have much of a choice in being alone. During one of the more challenging financial crisis in our lives, my wife needed to take a position several hours away from home. That meant that we would only get to see each other once a week for a day—if at all. It was a calculated move that was an investment in our future that required great sacrifice.

Unsure of how it was going to work, we reluctantly but necessarily embarked on the path, anticipating that it would be six months before she could transfer closer to home. Well, that six months turned into twelve, then twenty-four and eventually surpassed nine years.

Nine years.

Over the course of those years, our children moved out and the nest became empty. Throwing myself into work did not make up for the empty house I came home to each night. It didn't make up for the empty table I ate meals at alone, or the empty family room I sat in, or the empty bed I slept in alone.

The isolation was debilitating, which led to further isolation. It became suffocating and felt endless with no period of relief in sight. Isolating myself may have been one of the worst mistakes I ever made. I believe it directly contributed to the times I lost the will to live.

If you take away nothing else from this book, know that during times of crisis, it is of utmost importance to have a few close confidants in your circle to rely on for support. That support might come in the form of a brief phone call, an email, a text, or visit over a cup of coffee. I don't mean you have to go on for hours extolling your tales of woe. As a matter of fact, you may not talk about what's bothering you at all.

Connecting with someone may just be a refreshing break for you. These critical allies can help provide you with the much-needed boost to invigorate you to continue press forward. A crisis will certainly tell you who your friends are.

Breakthrough

Breakthroughs often occur at the place of your breaking point. They happen right after you hit bottom. When the pressure is so great that you surrender. When you give up trying to control the situation and instead embrace it.

I believe this is the watershed moment where we focus and align. We come to know in our hearts that there is more; things can be different; there is better. How? Because we let go. We release our grip because we either no longer have the strength, or we realize that the death grip on what we don't control is not serving us.

Imagining the possibilities and ability to achieve them can make them achievable. This happens not just once but on multiple occasions. It can occur at different times and for various reasons.

These breakthrough moments act as turbo boost, nitro injection launching pads that propel you into the orbit of your purpose. These are progressive moments along your path or journey. To leverage them it requires letting go of the resistance of disbelief and embracing the positive energy flow.

These powerful moments of momentum that occur should be leveraged to advance (if not catapult) forward progress. Like waves during high tide or a bike rolling downhill, use these moments to build up momentum.

Embrace and cherish them. Learn to capitalize on them.

Learn to ride the waves. Capture and put to good use the bountiful energy that comes from these breakthrough moments of clarity.

Creative stimulation can occur, blockages can clear, and floodgates can open. Here is where going with the flow is a good thing—it's the path of less resistance. Make conscious decisions to flow with the path of less resistance—not to be confused with the path of least resistance, which can be a moment of a distraction and is the easy way out.

This is not going along with others who believe it is too hard to go the route you should go. This is a prescriptive, desired, low-resistance path created with an acute focus on what you want. In other words, this is no accident.

This is by design—your design—based on what you wanted to happen. Maximize this turbo boost to its fullest potential to make significant steps and impact toward your goal. Block out the negative, progress-prohibiting thoughts that generally occur.

It takes far less effort to block out the contrary thoughts when focused on this stream. In other words, you must make the conscious decision and effort to concentrate on the negative for it to have an impact during these moments, unlike when you are in the normal flow of things.

MEANING

As I sat out on my back patio writing, I happened to look up and see a squirrel scurry up a tree and dart quickly from branch to branch. It stopped to chew on what appeared to be food, with its cheeks bulging out. All the while, its eyes searching for the next morsel. My gaze panned out to see the butterflies fluttering back and forth.

Off in the distance, the commanding blue jays were sailing from tree to tree, landing on branches as if to inspect the tree. They looked around the entire time, picking at the branch with their beaks a few times before fluttering off.

Out of the corner of my eye I noticed a giant frog, which blended in with the brownish-gray color of the exposed roots of the shrubbery. It stopped as I noticed it, remaining completely still. It looked around and then hopped again once when it decided it was safe to move. I watched this frog slowly progress through the shrubbery, one jump, stretch, and crawl at a time. It moved cautiously as it seemed to calculate whether each movement would catch food or help it avoid being food.

It occurred to me that these animals wake each day in search of food and are always on guard, trying to avoid being the meal. I wondered if they play. What is the purpose? Eat, poop, sleep, repeat. They don't have jobs, are not on a clock or schedule, and are certainly not seeking to amass stuff to impress others.

At that moment, I envied these creatures for their free-spiritedness. They didn't have to bear the weight of human responsibilities, except for the having-to-avoid-being-a-meal part. I pondered that there was probably a time when humans were the same way. Yes, an animal's existence can be defined as primitive: eat, sleep, poop, kill, avoid being killed, repeat. However, is this frantic human race to get, achieve, compete, or even crush a real purpose and true fulfillment?

If you stop to really think about it, there *has* to be a greater purpose than the pursuit of attaining stuff. What is the purpose of that? What is the motivation, and where does real, sustainable fulfillment come from? Certainly not in the acquisition, as that is a short-lived trophy. If attainment is for the purpose of helping others, of sharing or even giving, I could see fulfillment in striving to achieve as a means to an end.

Except for concerns of being eaten, these creatures didn't look worried or stressed. There is something to be said for and to learn from their way of life. Yes, of course there is the ecosystem and natural instinctive flow of the circle of life to take into consideration.

I am referring to the simple nature of existing without undue stress. Apart from the critical needs of food and rest, how important really is everything else? What priority does playfulness have in life?

Rarely did I see the creatures traveling in packs; we humans do differ in that human interaction and relationships, are also a primary need for a healthy disposition. I would put them right up there with food and rest. Again, apart from food, rest, and relationships, how much of a priority is stuff, really?

While thinking we could live with the simplicity of creatures far less developed than we are may be a bit idealistic and far-fetched, is there at least something we can extract from this? How out of balance do we become when we put a higher priority on the achievement of status or attaining material possessions over these basic needs?

PURPOSE: THE WHY

Actor Bill Murray has a line in the movie *St. Vincent* that says, "The tree was meant to give, so to be able to give everything and have nothing left is the best life the tree could ever have."

Money is tangible and temporary. It is not the be-all and end-all. There is another saying that goes:

> "It is not that money can't buy happiness,
> but rather that money cannot prevent sadness."
> —Anonymous

What can we find to give that outlasts the temporal things in life, that will make this world—our world—better off for us having been here? Is it a smile given to someone who has experienced the same loss we have? A hug offered to someone who has suffered as we have? An encouraging word spoken to someone who has been as discouraged as we have? Support for someone left out in the cold as we have experienced?

We have a profound ability to connect and relate to those who have traveled a similar journey as ours. We add to it from our unique perspectives as individuals that, when combined, can form a bond, a force that can help strengthen, heal, and grow. What can you give?

LOOKOUT POINTS

Along our path, we will inevitably encounter what I call lookout points. They are *challenge* and *turning points*.

Lookout points exist along scenic drives and hikes. The intent is to encourage the traveler to pause, take in and reflect, and perhaps alter their course. Challenge and turning points serve the same purpose.

Challenge points often precede turning points. They can occur and exist when we encounter mild difficulty up to the absolute unbearable. Either way, they force some type of movement to happen. At times of high pressure, the trial forces us to consider alternative paths, which we may not have been open to or may have resisted in the past.

These challenge points, when successfully navigated, can bring us to new heights that we may not have otherwise ventured to. When you reach a place of an extreme, pause for a moment and know that growth is occurring. It may be hard; you may even sweat, but know that it can result in being good for you. Unlike the overused business cliché "Never let them see you sweat," there comes a time when it is necessary. So sweat necessarily.

Don't falter or give up. Push through. Better to die trying than to go on living as a quitter. Here is where your indomitable will is forged.

Challenge points can evolve into turning points. That is where the road may not always be straight. Learn to recognize them. A turning point is when it is better to alter your course rather than proceed because the cost or danger ahead is greater than the benefit. Know when to downshift, course correct, or adjust your direction or speed while traveling on your journey.

Many times, these unexpected turns can lead to us reaching a better destination than the one we originally had in mind—if we remain open.

REASONS TO ENDURE

There are different reasons to endure. One reason may be a situation where you could have made better decisions, while another could be when you've done nothing wrong to bring the situation on yourself. In both cases, be aware of the tendency to continually beat yourself up over mistakes you may have made—and be careful not to do that. Acknowledge and embrace the error, learn from it to avoid repeating it, and then move on.

When things happen to us that we did not cause, we must also be careful not to blame or find fault with ourselves or accept the blame others may try to heap on us. Doing so will only serve to make enduring all that much more challenging —more weight to carry on our already-overloaded shoulders.

PERSPECTIVE

I once scratched the bumper of my brand-new car by backing into a pole while parking. It was one of the happiest days of my life.

I was taking my daughter Courtney to dinner at our favorite burger joint. During dinner, she told me that she had ended her relationship with a boyfriend who I really didn't care for. Rather than going off the deep end about him, I had known the best approach would be to allow her to experience and learn for herself. It was one of the most difficult things I've had to do as a parent, but necessary nonetheless.

Courtney told me she was not proud of her choice. She realized that she knew better, was raised better, and was more valuable than to be spending her life with this person. She said she had to learn that on her own. She was looking forward to getting on with her life and moving in a positive direction

Hearing those words of wisdom flowing from the mouth of my beautiful baby girl made me the happiest man on Earth that day. There are no words to describe the joy of that moment.

I purposely chose not to get the bumper fixed. Every time I look at it, it serves as a reminder of the very joyous moment on that very special day.

This is an example of how, if we choose, we can turn a

negative perspective into a positive one.

WHY ME?

Too often we talk ourselves out of our purpose, our vision, something good that we have the ability to accomplish. This happens when we are steeped in self-doubt and loathing. The fires of our passion for our dreams can be extinguished by doubt, fear, and feelings of low self-worth. "I've made many mistakes," we say. "I screwed up, waited too long." "I should have, could have, then I would have," also know as shudda, cudda, wudda disease.

It is critical to understand your purpose, what you are here to accomplish. Ask if it is for the greater good and in line with love, joy, and peace, and if your motives are in line.

Know the reason, and then remember: it's not for *you*. Know that your vision will benefit others beside yourself. Accomplishing this is not about and all for you.

When asking yourself if something is possible, remember that when for others' gains, not just our own, it is for them. We have a tendency to believe in and for others. We can easily see something good happening to someone else but not as easily for ourselves . . . especially if we have faced a string or history of challenges that have worn us down.

We often believe something it is possible for others but not for ourselves. Remember that it *is* for them. It is our gift to them and for them. If we can believe good things can happen for other people, then why can't we believe we can be that good thing—through our work, effort, dreams, visions, and existence? Having this mindset can help set the wheels in motion toward accomplishing our goals.

PACE YOURSELF

We all have a limited supply of energy to use on a daily basis. In some ways, it is like running a marathon. It is unwise to try (and not possible) to sprint the entire race. Once your energy is spent, its gone.

We must learn to temper the energy we expend, almost to the point of rationing it. There is time to use a burst and other times to use little. To be impactful and maintain peace, we must use our energy wisely and sparingly. Focus energy on the areas that matter and avoid wasting it on those that don't.

BECAUSE *WHEN* ENDS

When does *when* end? We don't always know the exact time, but we know that eventually it will.

I recall at time when going through cancer treatment when I was traveling to see my wife. As I pulled into the driveway, I saw Ben, the next door neighbor, poking around in his backyard. As I unloaded the trunk and set the alarm on my car, he poked his head up over the fence to ensure all was well. We spoke briefly and then both went on about our business. Just another run-of-the-mill day in both of our lives.

Within a month of that greeting, he was placed in hospice care as his stomach cancer had returned with a vengeance. Within a couple of months, Ben passed away. It happened so suddenly. I don't travel that way a lot, but each time I do, I still look for him to be meandering around in his backyard, cleaning the pool or fixing the fence or something. I still look for his long, weathered face, his square jaw and matter-of-fact, relaxed expression. I still look for him to say hi one more time. But that will never happen.

That same year, at a get-together for my wife's job, we were celebrating Rueben, a lucky co-worker who was transferring close to home. It was a small gathering of colleagues, spouses, partners, and friends in a cozy little restaurant. We had a chance to socialize with everyone in the intimate, relaxed setting outside.

When it came time to wrap up, we all said our good-byes. I

noticed the hug Rueben's wife gave my wife lasted just a little longer; her eyes welled up with tears during the exchange. Few words were spoken as she was apparently choked up, but her eyes told a story of pain and suffering, which I better understood later.

I didn't think much of it at the time; however, when I learned a couple of years later that Rueben's wife had passed away from cancer, I realized that parting had been the last good-bye. His wife had recently been diagnosed and was fighting, filled with hope, and she had a good chance of beating it. Maybe she knew, perhaps she was frightened; but in either case, as I look back, that was the last good-bye, which none of us expected.

We never truly know when a good-bye will be the last. When the hug will be the last embrace. We take for granted there will always be another. But life has a way of ending so abruptly, without notice, when we least expect it.

While we may grieve the loss, we should also be thankful for the life we were able to be a part of. The lost should also be a reminder to live our own lives to the fullest, each moment, hour, and day at a time.

Win

In every battle, there are wins and losses. The wins have a positive effect through encouragement. Having victorious and successful experiences is important for our confidence building and overall well-being.

Winning is recognizing and acknowledging our victories, no matter how small they might be. Keeping our heads down all the time in battle can be a living hell to endure day in and day out. The wins allow us to take a critical respite, bask in hope, and enjoy the satisfaction of a well-fought, endured struggle. This act revitalizes us for the next inevitable battle. Make a habit of counting and cherishing your wins.

YOU ARE THE GIFT

You are here for a reason. You have a purpose to fulfill. On most accounts, it involves someone other than yourself. I am convinced that you are here because what you have to offer or give is a gift. It may be one or it may be many gifts, but your purpose is a gift to others.

With that purpose in mind, remember: you don't go to the birthday party and not give the gift you were given to give.

When you look at your life and feel like giving up, feel like quitting, feel like *"Why bother?"* because you don't make a difference, I challenge you to look at things differently.

Know that every single one of us has a purpose, a reason to exist, a mission to fulfill. No one is a wallflower that doesn't matter unless we choose to be.

If we consider there are over 37 trillion cells in the human body, each of them serves a purpose. We know that it only takes one cell going rogue to create cancer. It's the healthy cells that combat and influence the bad ones that keep them from causing harm. We can look at ourselves as individual cells; yes, there are many, but each holds the ability to positively influence other cells or negatively infect them. If one in 37 trillion cells can have an impact, then certainly you as one of only seven billion people can make a difference.

So it does not matter what negative things your co-workers, friends, ex-friends, parents, siblings, relatives, boyfriends, girlfriends, husbands, wives, or enemies say about you. You *do* matter. I am here to tell you that you *do* make a difference, you *do* serve a purpose, and you *don't* get to give up and quit just because you think you don't matter. You need to deliver your package that has been assigned to you, and only you can provide it. You need to keep going no matter what.

When we look at problems, we should zoom out. We are in a building in a city or town, in a state, in a region, in a country. That country is on Earth in this galaxy that is one of the billions of galaxies in this universe. From that viewpoint, suddenly our big problems seem small in the grand scheme of things. This lens helps to put things into perspective.

Conversely, when we look at our purpose, we need to look at things in reverse, zooming back into the cell level. You can, you will make an impact; you are making one right now. Live your life. Be and give the gift you were meant to be.

CELEBRATE!

Be thankful. There is always, always, always something to be grateful for. One of the simplest and most effective ways to change your mood, energy, and circumstances is find something to be grateful for—and then repeat.

You may say, "Of course, there is, but I really don't feel like it right now. This problem I am facing is kicking my butt, and

I don't see how having a happy thought about something is going to change that."

My response is to remember that energy is like tuning into a radio station. The frequency you turn to is what you are going to hear. If you want to listen to rock, then don't tune into a classical station. Similarly, if you want to experience peace and joy, then don't tune into anger, malice or drama. What you tune into is what you get.

Simply put, you are going to get more of whatever your primary focus is on. If you have done all that you can, and there is nothing else you can do to fix your problem, then what is the harm in changing the channel to a different station? The worst that will happen is the positive impact of rest you will attain in taking a break from useless worrying while enjoying the gift of peace that comes from being thankful. Many times, the answer to your prayers, the solution you need, is there, in the place of peace, even in the eye of the storm. You will seldom find it embedded in the thick of the rapid movement and turmoil of battle. At times like these, you must be still to hear it.

Most of us have heard the story about the shoeless man who envied the man who had shoes until he met the man with no feet.

If we take a look around in our lives and make an honest assessment, we probably know of someone who is facing greater everyday challenges than we are. Some are even facing catastrophic challenges. If we are truthful with ourselves, we would not trade places with them, any of them. Yet they are still going on, living each day, not giving up.

The moral of the story is two-fold:
1. No matter what you might be dealing with, someone has it worse than you do.
2. Almost everything you are facing, someone else has

probably encountered it, and even worse.

In spite of it all, they persevered and made it through the crisis. If they did, so can you. We are not the first and, sadly, probably won't be the last to deal with the types of crises we face. We can, however, find peace in our walk, joy in our journey and success in our challenges—if we choose to.

Celebrate the victories; those are the challenges faced and overcome and the obstacles conquered. So are the preventive steps taken to capture and reject nonproductive thoughts as they occur.

FOCUS

Celebrate and cherish your enemies. I know this sounds odd, but think about it. Through their actions and behavior, they have actually helped you to Let Go, Live Now, and Win.

Rather than wasting negative energy heaping curses and ill will on your enemies, look at them as serving to providing resistance that is helping you to grow.

With this mindset, you can begin to welcome their resistance as you would a strength-training circuit. You can also opt to put down the weight (resistance) to rest and recuperate. Then pick it back up again and continue on your path of growth.

This resistance, properly leveraged, can help build up your resolve, focus, will, and even your determination. It can help you find a solution where you didn't see one before. Your detractors help you, so you should be thankful for them, not curse them.

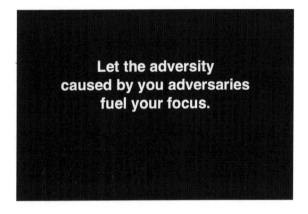

**Let the adversity
caused by you adversaries
fuel your focus.**

VICTORY

For as long as I can remember, my goal has been to "encourage the ordinary to find their extraordinary."

I recall an indescribably challenging time during my career where I encountered one of my greatest setbacks. What occurred and how I was being treated simply did not make sense to me. I had never felt more barely tolerated, unappreciated, and undervalued in my career.

The primary goal had been to build a phenomenal team from scratch, which I had accomplished, despite dealing with insurmountable obstacles and resistance.

I felt like I had been kicked in the teeth when I received feedback from my leadership team. Contrary to all other evidence, their perception was that I had failed.

As I sat in my office preparing to move to another assignment and fighting off sinking into deep despair, I assessed why I had even bothered if this was the end result. I questioned if investing in and helping others live up to their fullest potential was worth it. It appeared as though my trademark people-focused leadership style was not beneficial to my career but was instead a detriment. I began to question my purpose.

Just then I heard a soft knock at my office door. I looked up to see Ron, one of the employees on my team, standing in the doorway. He asked if I had a moment.

"Sure," I said, "come on in."

He entered hesitantly and slowly sat down, shoulders lowered. I could tell something was wrong by his body language.

He opened up the conversation with:

"I just heard the news. It is true?"

To which I responded:

"Yes, I am leaving."

"Wow, that is not right," he said. "When?"

"Today is my last day here."

"Mind if I close the door?" Ron asked

I shrugged yes.

He got up and closed the door. After he sat back down he said, "This is not something I would usually share at work or even feel comfortable sharing, but I might not have another chance."

He went on to share with me how his environment growing up had led him into a life he was not proud of. He'd moved here with pennies in his pocket to start a new life. When he first joined the company, he was living in a rehab facility.

He described what he went through each day he was living there. How the enforced discipline meant he would find his entire room turned upside down if one thing was out of order. How unsettling his rotation of sometimes questionable and unsavory roommates was. How at night he would be in fear for his life because of a new roommate. How some were later incarcerated, and others enjoyed the art of self-branding with a coat hanger. How he arrived home from work one day to a busy crime scene where another resident had taken his own life by drinking bleach. He never knew what he would come home to each day.

He said that this job—specifically my investing in him through coaching and development—was the only thing that provided him stability in his life. During his personal struggle, he had lost eight friends to suicide or overdose. Most days during the early years, it was all he could do to hold himself together.

He told me that he felt his story might change my opinion of him. He thought he would be risking his career by sharing this type of information because it was outside the traditional boundaries of regular work talk. However, he felt it was more important for me to know the impact I had made on his life . . . that if it wasn't for me, he might not still be here, as in alive.

I was quite moved by his story, to the point of being shaken. I thought *What if I had given up? What if I had quit? What if I didn't care about people, didn't invest in them, in Ron? He might not be here today, and I would never have known.*

This situation permanently impressed upon me that we have in impact on others that we may never know of. Fortunately, I was able to hear it first hand, but what about the times we don't?

All that I had been feeling just moments prior—all the bad, all the regret, all the angst, all the disappointment—dissipated. While I may not have realized the reward in my career at that company, a much greater purpose had been accomplished. It was clear that my purpose had been served, my goal achieved.

That was fulfilling beyond measure. I had living proof that the suffering, challenge, and pain were all worth it. One life had been positively impacted. It was as if the universe was telling me, "See, all is not lost. Your efforts have not been wasted. Stay true to yourself, your principals, your purpose."

What I had endured, which initially appeared to be the agony of defeat, turned instead into an experience of one of my greatest victories. I *won* that battle.

YOUR STORY

In learning to live, you should make the effort to discover and know your story.

What's your story?
What makes you tick?
Why?
What do you want your legacy to be?

I don't mean someone else's story, but your story that you have created or are creating. While your crisis is not unique, you are. How will you leverage, recycle, repurpose your journey to make something out of it? That is always an option. This self-examination will help you find your purpose to go on.

LIVE INTENTIONALLY

Now go and live your best life, with intent—one moment at a time.

Battle Arsenal for Endurance

In the remaining pages you will find insight, tips, and thought-provoking narratives. Their purpose is intended to help guide and support you through endurance in crisis. They are arranged by topic and do not require following a specific order. Feel free to read in any order you chose. If you prefer to jump to a subject that particularly interests you, by all means, go ahead. The idea is that you can read and refer to them as needed and as often as necessary, and hopefully you'll extract a nugget or two to help you along your journey. Consider these mini compositions on perspective as a mental arsenal, intended for encouragement to help support and sustain during your mission. In short, they are endurance strategies.

THOUGHTS

Change your thoughts and change your world.
—Norman Vincent Peale

A mind is a powerful tool that can also be a destructive weapon. Which result depends on how we allow our minds to engage. How often do we kill dreams, goals and passionate pursuits in our head before they have a chance to birth? If we allow our thoughts to replay continually the negative, more than likely, that will snowball into an erosion of our energy and hope. Worse, over long periods, negative thoughts become a strength and creativity sapping vortex. Negative thoughts feed off of and spawn other negative thoughts, stifling the right ones. On the other hand, positive thoughts both negate the negative ones while helping to encourage and inspire growth. Which thought process are you feeding right now?

Your thoughts will eat you alive if you feed them.

TRY

It's hard to fail, but it is worse never to have tried to succeed.
—Theodore Roosevelt

Failure can be hard to take. Repeated failure can cause us to avoid even trying. Success does not happen by accident or on its own. It does not happen in every case, but rest assured, for it to happen, we must, at the very minimum, first attempt.

> **Failure is guaranteed
> if we quit.
> Success is always negotiable
> if we at least try.**

SEEDS

Someone is sitting in the shade today because someone planted a tree a long time ago.

—Warren Buffett

There are times in our struggles when we ask, "Why bother?" or "What's the point?" especially when we are battling and don't see the results. In fact, it seems like all we ever see is defeat. Yes, the challenge may be hard right now, and you may not see a light at the end of the tunnel, but keep on going anyhow. The things that we do for an intended purpose, for the greater good, are like planting seeds. We may not ever see the results firsthand and need to learn to be okay with that—shifting from selfish to selfless.

Know that at some point someone will appreciate your sacrifice. They will win because you didn't quit. They will be comforted from your pain. They will experience rest from your efforts. Keep sowing and planting. Persevere until you see the light at the end of the tunnel—I promise you, it's not a train. You are here for a reason. What seeds are you planting today?

OBSTACLES

When obstacles arise, you change your direction to reach your goal;
you do not change your decision
to get there.
—Zig Ziglar

When we set out to make a positive difference, one of the most powerful things we can do is to decide. When we make up in our minds that "We will [fill in the blank] to improve [fill in the blank]," it sets in motion the course and momentum needed to achieve the goal. We may—we will—encounter resistance. However, being armed with the map of the decision, we can always refer back to it and look for a different path if the obstacle truly calls for a course correction. To get where we want to go, we may need to shift left or right; we may need to climb up and over or dig under. There are even times when we must venture straight forward unknowing, like driving in a thick cloud of fog, trusting in faith that we will be okay. During these times, even though we cannot see success in the present, we can stay the course because we know we have seen it inside. The good in all of this is that there is progress, movement, and advancement toward our goal.

The one thing we don't do when faced with opposition is change our decision. We stand firm, even if that is all we can do. We maintain a resolve and an impenetrable determination that we will rise, we will emerge, we will see victory. Know that even if all we can do is stand (still believing), by that very act we send a message to our adversaries that says, "While I may not be there yet, you haven't defeated me; I'm still standing!"

LIFE

The whole of life is but a moment of time. It is our duty, therefore to use it, not to misuse it.

—Plutarch

What if one morning you woke up and someone had deposited $86,400 into your bank account with the only caveat being that you must spend every penny of it that day and that day only? Well, I've got great news for you! Each and every one of us gets 86,400 seconds to spend each day—how we spend them is our choice.

Even with life spans increasing thanks to modern science, the number of 86,400 portions are not infinite in this world—in fact, they are limited. You must ask yourself, just as if you were spending your own money, is it worth spending this 20,000 seconds being upset over something I have absolutely no control over? Will using 30,000 seconds to gossip, spew hate, or mindlessly do nothing serve a purpose and make me feel like that was time well spent? What am I going to get in exchange for wasting 40,000 seconds dwelling on being offended by something someone said to me? Like using a slot machine in Vegas, you will probably put another 40,000 in trying to win back the original 40,000. But life doesn't quite work that way.

If we look at our lives as an investment on a second-by-second basis, and we choose to use our valuable seconds on things that matter, that makes a difference, the result will become part of our lasting legacy long after we have used up all of our allotted seconds. That is a life well spent.

By the way, with more time, you can get more money, but you can't use money to increase or buy back the 86,400 seconds—to get more time. So I ask you, how are you using your 86,400 seconds today?

COURAGE

Real courage is when you know you're licked before you begin, but you begin anyway and see it through no matter what.

—Harper Lee

How many times have you faced mountains so high, challenges so big, that by appearance there was no way you would be able to conquer them, so you just gave up? Now, have you ever gone forward anyway, whether you meant to or not, against impossible odds, even once, and emerged victorious? Or at a minimum, wound up better off than where you began?

If not, you should. All it takes is once. Yes, we may encounter defeat repeatedly, but what can actually occur during those experiences can strengthen, not weaken, us. We can use defeat to build up a resistance to disappointment rather than an acceptance of it. The human will is powerful beyond imagination. We, you and I, can get to the point where we feel like our backs are up against the wall, but if we can muster the courage to move forward in spite of whatever obstacles we may face, there will be a breakthrough, a victory obtained. It is always there—but it's up to us to go and get it! Failure is guaranteed if we quit.

Success is always negotiable if we at least try.

**Failure is guaranteed
if we quit.
Success is always negotiable
if we at least try.**

PREPARATION

To be prepared for war is one of the most effective means of preserving peace.
—George Washington

Preparation is a proven strategy deployed by powerful nations as a way of fortifying and protecting its territories. We can also apply this to our own lives.

If you have ever chosen to embark on doing something good, making things better, pursuing a dream, or trying to make a difference, especially when it involves serving or benefiting others, you know that there is always plenty of opposition.

There are always opposing forces, regardless of whether it makes sense or if there should be. Things, events, and people will seem to go out of their way in what may appear to be efforts to make you fail instead of succeed. These are distractions.

If we wish to maintain peace in the midst of our battles, we must prepare by arming and equipping ourselves with the robust arsenal needed to endure. At a minimum, we need to be armed with belief, hope, faith, perseverance, discipline, stamina, grit, acceptance, surrender, forgiveness, and focus.

In the same way that we prepare to face inclement weather when venturing outdoors, or the obstacles we will face when climbing a mountain, we need to prepare to face the inevitable resistance we will encounter as we pursue our dreams in life. It is never easy, but by being prepared, we can have peace during our pursuit.

Let the adversity caused by your adversaries fuel your focus.
—Nate Battle

DESTINY

Destiny is no matter of chance. It is a matter of choice: It is not a thing to be waited for, it is a thing to be achieved.
—William Jennings Bryan

Words and phrases often used when defining destiny include *predetermined, inevitable, lot in life,* or *fortune.* Make no mistake: accidental or by chance are not acceptable options when identifying and going after our chosen destiny.

Effort, belief, action, faith, focus, hard work and an indomitable determination are. The common theme among these attributes is choice. We achieve our destiny by the choices we make.

Today, right now, choose: decide to go after what you want, what you know to be inside of you that you must accomplish before you leave this earth. Put fear and past defeat aside—yes, take a chance by making a choice.

We decide our destiny by our determination— dare to be determined.
—Nate Battle

THINK BIG

Whatever you're thinking, think bigger.
—Tony Hsieh

Think big is sage advice in the business world where there is a perpetual quest for bigger, brighter, and better. This has an even greater impact, however, when we apply it to our lives . . . especially when we take into account that our thoughts determine our actions, behavior, and, ultimately, our results.

A recipe for growth and peace:

- When tempted to be critical of or to attack someone's behavior, think bigger. Rise above that small mindset and be more tolerant of behavior you consider unbecoming. Instead, emulate the behavior you would like to see.
- When you think you cannot achieve something, think bigger, as in a mind-blowing version of your goal— and then go for it! You will amaze yourself by what you are capable of accomplishing. In the worst-case scenario, you will likely achieve greater than the original goal you set out to accomplish.

- When tempted to become angry with someone or something petty, think bigger. You have so much potential, so much to accomplish, such greatness within you. Is it really worth wasting an ounce of energy or a moment of time on something that, in the grand scheme of things, just does not matter?

These are just a few examples. The more we expand our thinking, the more our minds, lives, and worlds expand. In practice, when we feel our thoughts getting small . . . Think Bigger!

How tragic to live only in a finite space in an infinite world.
—Nate Battle

CHANGE

If we don't change, we don't grow.
If we don't grow, we are not really living.
Growth demands a temporary surrender of security.
-—Gail Sheehy

Change can be scary. It has a tendency to frighten us because it usually means letting go of something we are familiar and comfortable with in exchange for something we are not. This is true even when what we have is not what we want, is uncomfortable, or is possibly even painful. We are still willing to hold on to it because we think a change might be worse.

How can we possibly grow if we refuse to change? We don't read the same books, play with the same toys, or wear the same clothes we did when we were children— because we grew. In fact, we had a desire to grow, expand, experience. How tragic would it be if we had the capacity and aptitude to do great things but chose not to in order to remain toddlers? That would not be natural.

We instinctively cloak ourselves in the false security of the familiar, thinking it will protect us, when in fact, that thing, habit, person, job, living situation, or toxic relationship (that we are familiar with, yet still drains us) is causing more harm than good.

We must be willing to surrender the hindrance in order to grow. *Surrender* here meaning to let go, yield, give up, and even abandon. As challenging as that may sound, try not to focus as much on the object but on the power it has over you. That is what we surrender—the oppressive power. Surrendering and being open to change enables us to be able to say, "This [fill in the blank] no longer has power over me to influence, harm, or rob me of my peace and joy." We must be honest with ourselves in asking, "Is something that is harming me in this way truly offering security?"

With that new frame of mind, let go of what you cannot control and have faith that what will come in its place will be better for you and will restore your peace. Growth is not easy, but it's worth the effort. How will you grow today?

"Do not wait until the conditions are perfect to begin. Beginning makes the conditions perfect."
—Alan Cohen

EXPERIENCE

Experience is a hard teacher because she gives the test first, the lesson afterward.

—Vernon Sanders Law

Have you ever struggled with feeling like you are failing rather than passing tests in life? Take heart. That is, in some ways, by design.

How many times in school or work, when we were allowed or required to take a test a second time, did we do better? Especially when we recalled the first time we went through it?

Wisdom is the application of knowledge. Knowledge comes from a textbook, while wisdom comes through experience.

Rather than feeling down or disheartened over what you might see as failure, look at it as a test. Look for the message and learning that you can extract from the situation. That way you will be ready to apply it next time around. Hint: in life, we get to repeat some tests until we pass.

If you are looking to grow and make forward progress, cherish the learning from tests you didn't pass and the related experience. This will help you succeed in life. The experience is priceless and provides knowledge that no one can ever take away from you. Ready? Set? Fail. Learn! Grow! Repeat.

NO HATE

Why I refuse to hate:

When you love someone:
- when you hear their name, it causes an emotional reaction.
- when you hear their voice, it causes an emotional reaction.
- when you think of them, it causes an emotional reaction.

When you hate someone:
- when you hear their name, it causes an emotional reaction.
- when you hear their voice, it causes an emotional reaction.
- when you think of them, it causes an emotional reaction.

Why would I give someone I don't care for the same focus and attention that I give someone whom I love?

This is why I refuse to hate.

GET BUSY

Nobody makes a greater mistake than he who does nothing because he could only do a little.

—Edmund Burke

How many times have we sat back and hesitated or just flat out didn't even try because we thought, "What difference would it make anyway?"

Too often this is the case when we are overwhelmed by the challenge or effort that we are presently facing. By appearance, what stands before us seems insurmountable or would take far more effort than we could ever give or have in us; or so we think.

Every victory began with a single step. In fact, the greatest victories required the most steps. In order to be able to reach the goal of achievement, the steps need to be taken.

Rather than looking at and focusing on all the steps, actions, or elements that you think need to occur before you can achieve what you desire, break your challenge down into individual steps. Resolve to proceed in spite of how high the hill may seem, and then take a step, and then another, and then another.

At the very least you will be farther along than where you were before, which was stuck. As a bonus, you may find that you inspire yourself and others along that way.

Rather than focusing on how many steps you have ahead of you, glance back to remember and be grateful for the many steps you have successfully taken, while remaining focused on the step, action, or effort you need to take next. You probably didn't think you would make it this far, but you did—so continue on.

Know that you are not alone in this journey. Have faith that if it is in your heart to achieve it, some good will come out it. Each step, no matter how many or how hard, is worth it. Now get to steppin'!

I would rather risk dying trying to live than to live on as a quitter who refused to try.

—Nate Battle

COMPLACENCE

Most everything that you want is just outside your comfort zone.
—Jack Canfield

The quote above has been paraphrased in any number of different ways. Yet another would be to exchange the words *comfort* with *complacence* of the attributes comfort and complacence share are reassuring, soothing, and pleasant. Sometimes they apply to one's own accomplishments and status. These become the boundaries of our limiting zone of complacence.

There is a noticeable absence of any resistance in our zone of complacence. The resistance we face is often an indicator of progress.

We need to ask ourselves what we are willing to give up that is familiar and comfortable and that we are accustomed to dealing with to instead have what we really want.

Point blank, if we want peace, it may mean that we must temporarily part with what is tolerable in order to face, address, and remove the challenging obstacles that lie in the path to true peace.

To be and feel whole may mean letting go of the

stronghold we have on the unforgivingness that we have become comfortable with (whether within ourselves or toward others), and stretching ourselves (read: feeling uncomfortable) to give forgiveness.

Beyond material things, what is it that you truly want? What are you willing to let go of (that you are comfortably holding on to) in order to make room and be able to receive and hold it with the very hand with which you are holding your present comfort?

Our world of opportunities exists and expands through the resulting un-comfortableness that comes from pushing past our self-imposed boundaries.

In order to grow, what comfort are you going to let go of today?

When the pain of the present becomes greater than fear of the future that is when real growth begins to take place.

—Nate Battle

POTENTIAL

This "eye chart" hangs on the wall in my office as one of my favorites.

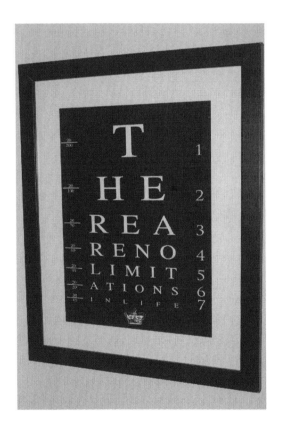

It speaks volumes in its dual message, the same way it

spoke to me in the store.

To see the message contained within, you must look at things in a different way than you may be used to looking at them. To understand its message, you are required to focus and take time to study it. You must go outside of your mental boundaries and let go of your restrictive thinking.

If we shift our focus, the reward is a message that is profoundly true as it relates to potential.

Hint—our potential is endless. Especially when we seek to emanate love, joy, peace, patience, and kindness.

MISTAKES

You are going to make mistakes in life. It's what you do after the mistakes that counts.

—Brandi Chastain

One of the best statements I've heard is, "It's not what happens to us in life, but how we respond to it that matters." If we are attempting to do something positive, trying to make an impact, a difference, inevitably we are going to make mistakes. We might be sincere in our desire and effort; however we may at times be sincerely wrong.

Other times we allow ourselves to be led by that detracting inner voice, the other one whose sole purpose is to distract us and get us off track, off our path.

As my mom once said to me: When you hit rock bottom, there is nowhere to go but up. To which I added: The velocity at which we hit rock bottom determines the momentum at which we travel up!

Be encouraged. Our mistakes are actually gifts that provide us with experience, albeit uncomfortable. More importantly, they become unforgettable experiences. We can choose to learn from them, and then they will stay with and help us for the rest of our lives.

Not trying, to avoid mistakes, is like not eating, to avoid gaining weight. Don't kill your dream by not feeding it.

—Nate Battle

PROBLEMS

*Often in life, the most important question we can ask ourselves is: do
we really have the problem we think we have?*

—Sheri Fink

Natural disasters like earthquakes, tornados, hurricanes, and tsunamis are without question real problems. There are also occasions in our lives when we face crises that can be defined as unnatural. Apart from these instances, can we truly be in a constant state of dilemma? Is every matter that gives us cause for concern a problem, or is the problem in the perception—our perception?

If we are honest with ourselves, and we stop to carefully examine whatever we are facing at the present moment—that thing that is bothering us—we may find that the "problem" may not be exactly as we imagine it to be.

The mind is an incredible resource. The limits of its creative capacity and capability have yet to be fully determined. With the mental power of a locomotive, its abilities are that of a true workhorse going nonstop. However, similar to the train engine, in the absence of the engineer and conductor to drive and steer on a determined path along the tracks, great destruction can occur. In other words, if left up to its own, the mind can wreak havoc like a runaway train.

As humans, we possess the ability to think things into existence—good, bad, or otherwise. As essayist James Allen once said, "As a man thinketh, so is he." How many of our problems exist entirely in our heads as opposed to the real obstacles before us? Then, of the actual obstacles, how many of them are actually insurmountable?

The battle is often won or lost in the mind before any physical action ever takes place. If we proactively move our battle position from reacting to thoughts to a preventive position of capturing and rejecting thoughts at their first occurrence that do not serve us , we will find our problems shrink. We will either see that we can overcome them, or they will simply dissolve like the mirages they are, mirages we allowed to prevent us from making forward progress.

Master your mind, your thoughts, to remove distracting illusions, and then rule your problems.

To prevent a toxic thought from defeating you, reject and then eject it.
—Nate Battle

WAITING

Don't wait. The time will never be just right.
—Napoleon Hill

How often do we "when"? When the time is right. When this happens. When that is in place.

If we are completely honest with ourselves, most of the time we already know what we need to do at this moment. While we may not exactly know what we need to do in the future, we do know what needs to be done— what step, action, effort we need—now! But instead, we use "when" as an excuse, a crutch, and reason to procrastinate, to avoid doing what we know we must do.

Our reasoning varies. We may view what we need to do as too painful, too hard, or just not fun. Regardless, in order to progress and grow, we must face and do what needs to be done no matter how challenging it may appear. Too often, the decision to act is the hardest part.

The next time you encounter one of those "when" moments, to help determine priorities ask yourself, "What would I do if this were my last day on earth?"

CAN DO

Do not let what you cannot do interfere with what you can do.
—John R. Wooden

How often do we stop in our tracks, paralyzed and overwhelmed or in fear of something we have zero ability to change? We allow an apparent obstacle to prevent us from making progress, thinking that it is an impenetrable barrier.

It's like giving up after the great oak doesn't fall after one blow from the axe. To the rock, a single drop of water poses little threat. However, over time, drop after drop, day after day, year after year, the "impenetrable" rock will eventually begin to wear down.

Our focus and efforts need to continually be on what we *can* do—what we *can* accomplish. This serves two purposes. First, we make continual progress toward our goal by wearing down the resistance one step, act, and moment at a time. Second, it is a source of motivation. With progress comes the reward of a reminder that we *can* do this or we *can* do that. These individual victories, when combined, help form the current that flows within us and helps us to keep going.

KNOWING

I know for sure that what we dwell on is who we become.
—Oprah Winfrey

There is great power in thought. It has been said that thought is an energy, like a magnetic force. It attracts like energy. Some have gone so far as to say what you think about most is your god.

To dwell is to linger or stay. How often have we dwelled on something negative, obsessing about it continually and eventually seeing it come to pass? We are not surprised when it happens. What if I told you that you were the driving force in making something happen?

What if, instead of focusing on what we *don't* want, we change our focus to something we *do* desire?

That is not to say we want our enemies to all jump off a cliff. We want instead to remain engrossed in our purpose, being so fulfilled that we barely notice our enemies existence.

The image we see through the lens of the binoculars we hold is the one we aim at and focus on.

Want to change your life for the better? Change your focus as each thought occurs—one thought, one moment, at a time. We instinctively become the product of our environment. Where you live mentally eventually determines that you will assuredly become what you dwell on.

You can read the words, you can write them down, you can repeat them, you can recite them and share them with others but not until you believe them do they become true.

—Nate Battle

GOALS

*The tragedy in life doesn't lie in not reaching your goal. The tragedy
lies in having no goal to reach.*
—Benjamin Mays

We often hear the advice to "follow your passion." The
next important step after deciding to follow your passion
is to pursue your purpose. It is a journey, an effort aimed
at achieving a particular goal. It will be something you are
passionate about. Hint, it will benefit others beyond just
yourself.

Purpose serves to create and put substance behind a
tangible and impactful legacy, while passion alone can exist
as just a dream. Passion is an emotion that on its own may
not accomplish much. Purpose is not a feeling; it is the
reason for, the intent of, the determination to achieve the
goal. Passion acts as the fuel for the mission.

*A goal is a destination point along our journey without which we are
merely traveling aimlessly.*
—Nate Battle

EFFORT

There's an old saying that goes,

"If it's gonna be, it's up to me."

Work as if everything depends on you, and believe as if everything depends on your faith, what you know in your heart to be true.

CHARACTER

Character may be manifested in great moments, but it is made in the small ones.

—Phillips Brooks

I imagine character as a strong brick wall, a fortress of sorts. That fortress is built to stand up against those things that challenge us, that seek to diminish our worth and value through attempts to erode our integrity.

As with any constructed brick structure of quality, strong walls are built one brick or stone at a time. The impact and benefit of the focus, care, and craftsmanship that goes into skillfully placing each block in place is not seen until the wall is tested.

Look at each test, challenge, and opposition as an opportunity to cement another brick in your character structure. That's simply how it's done. Take the stones that are thrown at you and use them to build up your strength of character. Then, when the winds and storms of challenge arise, you will be able to withstand them, emerging with an unscathed and increased quality of character.

To forge your mental and moral qualities, your

character excellence, courageously build it one brick, one stone, one moment at a time.

> *Our true colors bleed out during crisis.*
> —Nate Battle

FALLING DOWN

You're going to fall down, but the world doesn't care how many times you fall down, as long as it's one fewer than the number of times you get back up.

—Aaron Sorkin

In this life, we are going to trip, stumble, and even fall. Not just once but repeatedly. In fact, the more you try to accomplish, achieve, make an impact, or make a difference the more you will stumble and, yes, fall.

Our human nature is to judgmentally categorize these as failures and continually replay them in our minds. This often results in a defeated spirit that gives in to the internal voice that antagonizes us with its sultry tone, with murmurs of "Why even try anymore; why bother? You're just going to fall again. You failed before, so what makes you think you won't again? Just give up already."

Put bluntly, that voice, not you, is an idiot. It should not be listened to—ever. For clarity, the definition of *idiot* here is "utterly foolish or senseless." That voice serves no other purpose but to persuade you away from persevering. To distract you from accomplishing what you know you were meant—predestined, even—to accomplish during your short time here on Earth.

If you feel like you have tripped and fallen, I challenge you to pick yourself up, dust yourself off, and stand tall. The dusting-off process is the acknowledgment of the fall and the act of separating yourself from the residue of that fall.

The sweeping motion of the dusting is the determination (will) to move on and away from it with the intent of not falling again. Take each step for what it is: a present step toward your future and one more step away from your past, which you need to let go of. Then repeat.

Inevitably, you will fall again. It will feel awful. You will get tired. You will feel like quitting—but don't. If all you can do is muster enough strength to stand in defiance, then stand. Be still, and know that you have won.

"The earth is round and the place which may seem like the end may also be the beginning"

—*Ivy Baker Priest*

COURAGE

Courage doesn't mean you don't get afraid.
Courage means you don't let fear stop you.
—Bethany Hamilton

One definition of courage is "the quality of mind or spirit that enables a person to face difficulty, danger, pain, etc., without fear; bravery."

One could interpret this as the absence of fear. I would challenge you, however, to look at it differently. If we make up in our mind and spirit to face whatever challenge is before us, walking directly toward it with the intent to walk through it regardless of the outcome—that is indeed courage. We refuse to allow fear to stop us; we defy it instead. "Without fear" is because of our choice to leave fear behind, deciding not to take it with us. It may still be there, but we left it and instead chose courage. Determined, we walk forward. Opt to abandon fear for courage.

KNOCKED DOWN

They tried to bury us.
They did not know we were seeds.
—Mexican Proverb

I love the quote above because it is another way to view getting knocked down to the ground. The seed needs and uses the ground (soil) to grow. Being knocked down can, in a sense, help us become more grounded, balanced, and sensible. If we choose, we can leverage resistance (from obstacles and setbacks) as the seed uses the soil: to help us grow stronger. With that shift in focus, instead of cursing them, we can celebrate our enemies and cherish the gifts they bring us. Les Brown said it best: "When you get knocked down, try to fall on your back. Because if you can look up, you can get up!" Press forward, stay the course, and don't you dare give up . . . no matter what.

Where you are now may not be where you want to be, but may lead
to where you want to be.
—Nate Battle

DECIDING

I am not a product of my circumstances.
I am a product of my decisions.
—Stephen R. Covey

An interpretation of this quote can be that who you are and where you are at in life is because of the decisions you have made, good, bad, or otherwise. This can be a bitter pill to swallow if you are not yet who you want to be. Once you embrace and get past that, the good news is that who you are is not dictated by your circumstances or luck.

We possess the ability to directly influence and become who we want to be. That comes through the power of decisions. We all know the impact of our poor decisions, but let's not linger there. Good decisions have an even greater impact—but we must first make them. When we finally grow tired of being driven and pushed around by life, and we take back the reins through deciding, we change our circumstances instead of letting them change us. Change starts with a decision. If not now, when?

RESISTANCE

Little minds are tamed and subdued by misfortune; but great minds rise above them.
——Washington Irving

Research shows the brain is like a muscle. We know that muscle grows and gets stronger with practice. That practice comes in the form of resistance. If we consider whatever we are facing or going through, and experiencing whatever trials, challenges, setbacks, and outright battles we are fighting as resistance, then if we endure by choice, the result is an enlarged mind. A mind that is more capable, prepared, and ready to face and handle the next challenge. A mind more skilled in dealing with ease with challenges once thought to be large. With a shift in perspective, we can look upon what we face, regardless of its size, as an opportunity and be thankful for it. This shift to a practice of gratitude will also help give us strength to endure.

You are strong—press on!

Avoiding perceived pain will not prevent it, but instead create a perpetual purgatory.
—Nate Battle

PERSPECTIVE

A pessimist sees difficulty in every opportunity; an optimist sees the opportunity in every difficulty.
—Winston Churchill

Life is about perspective. What we look for, we see. What we see, we tend to focus on. What we focus on, we attract more of. Change your perspective, change your day, change your life.

There was a story I once heard about twin boys. There were extreme opposites as one was on optimist and the other a pessimist. Their parents sought the help of a psychologist to help them adjust their perspective.

They agreed to an experiment to try and temper their dispositions. They put the pessimist son in a room with a brand new bicycle. He responded by saying "Oh great, I'll probably fall and skin my knee on this bike."

In the other room where they put the optimistic son, they heard shouts of joy and elation. The had placed only a box of manure in his room. He was digging in the manure throwing it everywhere. The psychologist asked him what he was so happy. The boy exclaimed, "Wha-hoo! With all this poop, there's gotta be a pony in here somewhere!"

In life, regardless of the circumstance,   look for the pony.

You will not get what you desire by focusing on what you don't want.
—Nate Battle

GOAL

A goal is not always meant to be reached, it often serves simply as something to aim at.
—Bruce Lee

At times we get discouraged because the goal we set out to conquer is not achieved exactly as we had hoped or planned. Sometimes defeat occurs when we run into the first obstacle that indicates our goal, as we see it, may not be attainable in the way we foresee achieving it.

Know that the curves, bumps, detours, and potholes along the road to our goal often serve a purpose—to strengthen our resolve and help us to focus.

We can benefit greatly by being open to adapting our journey and willing to adjust our course. Sometimes there may be lessons along the way that will help us get to where we had envisioned in a better way—if we are willing to listen.

Other times, our vision may have been too small or limited. Be aware of the obstacles while being receptive to the message they may be trying to enlighten you with. You may find that there exists a much greater opportunity than the one you first sought to achieve.

In reality, there is no "arrival," even with goal attainment. Once we reach the plateau after having scaled our mountain, we gain awareness that there is always more to see, do, and experience through the expanded view that comes with our new experience.

More important than goal attainment is starting. After setting your goal and creating a plan, step out and pursue it. From there, continue to relentlessly press forward, remembering to enjoy the journey with a positive anticipation of greatness; you won't be disappointed.

We cannot change the past but we can learn from it. We cannot control the future but should plan for it.

—Nate Battle

SUCCESS

Success is not just what you accomplish in your life, it is about what you inspire others to do.

—Anonymous

Success is about inspiring others.

Imagine if you built a business and sold it for hundreds of millions of dollars; or you won the lottery— the big one, so money became no object. You could afford every material thing your heart desires— everything.

Imagine yourself being on an island. Not a small island but one the size of a large city. A place with winding roads, sprawling hills, with land as far as the eye can see. One that has lavish views of the landscape adorned with grand estates. You have at your disposal every amenity and convenience known to man. Every material possession you could possibly think of.

Now imagine that you were completely alone. Not another human being on your island with you. No one to share your wealth with, to talk to, laugh with, to enjoy a simple meal with. How long before this would become old, unfulfilling, even unbearable?

While it may appear on the surface that attaining

"stuff" from our accomplishments is the be-all and end-all, it is not. In our pursuit, the questions to ask ourselves are: Why? What is the purpose? What impact have I made or will I make in pursuing this accomplishment? The answer should include more than just benefiting ourselves. Remember the island?

And by the way, inspiring others does not require wealth—it's free.

What is success? It is being able to go to bed each night with your soul at peace"
—Paulo Coelho

MAKING A DIFFERENCE

Each day when I awake I know I have one more day to make a difference in someone's life.
—James Mann

"What's the point?" you may ask. What is the meaning? Same old daily routine. Just more of the same today that happened yesterday. You may be feeling like you are walking in place. Unable to shake that all-too-familiar feeling of stagnation. Perhaps it's the feeling of hopelessness in your present situations that persists, despite your best efforts to change them. Why bother, you may ask—assuming nothing will ever change.

Why? Because it's not all about you. We are who we are and where we are for a reason. While not necessarily known to us all the time, we each have a profound impact on the people with whom we cross paths.

One way that is certain to change our disposition of complacency, unrest, and even defeat is to shift our focus away from ourselves and toward others who may be in need. To be specific, I'm not talking about money.

What is the cost of a smile? A kind word for no other reason than just because. What do we stand to lose by lending an ear to listen without judging? What does it cost us to provide someone who may be hurting with a few moments of respite where they can let their guard down, speak freely, and be heard. What is the value of an encouraging word spoken about someone's strength to counter the many weakness people are quick to point out?

In a word: Priceless! That act, thoughtful gesture, or warm smile might just be the best part of someone else's day. If you find yourself in a rut, wondering what's the use, or just over it all, try a change in focus. Look for an opportunity to be to someone else what you would want someone to be to you—a light in a sometimes-dark place. I dare you.

Often our most potent passionate presence comes from our deepest point of pain.
—Nate Battle

PROGRESS

If there is no struggle, there is no progress.
—Frederick Douglass

When the pain of the present becomes greater than the fear of the future, real change and progress begin to take place.

It is during these painful moments either through courage or sheer desperation, that we move. When our present state, our current situation, our utter existence has become more uncomfortable, even unbearable; when we say to ourselves, "Trying cannot be any worse than this," that is when we move.

It is during moments like these that we experience breakthroughs. By letting go of our habitual stronghold on 'what is' and being willing and open to accepting, embracing and walking towards something new, something different.

Often, it is the very thing we desire, our sense of purpose, our calling. That persistent voice inside of us that has been prompting us to pursue our destiny, but we are too afraid.

Why? Because as long as our dream remains a dream,

it remains possible—and that give us hope. But once we pursue it, we risk finding out it may not be achievable. So we continue on, in our safe place, with what we are familiar with, despite being unfulfilled. That wretched place of no change - until we can no longer bear it.

By letting go and banishing the fear that has held us captive, we actually experience freedom. What is it that you stand to lose, versus what you stand to gain?

When the pain of the present becomes greater than the fear of the future that is when real change and progress begin to take place.

—Nate Battle

BEACH PEACE

One day while attempting to spend some quality time with nature, to relax and be at peace at one of my favorite secluded spots, my picturesque view of the ocean and quiet enjoyment were suddenly, shall I say, eclipsed by two people.

I contemplated my options. I could say something like, "Excuse me," uncertain if the attempt at a polite resolution would be lost on my two visitors who appeared to lack the discernment of spacial awareness (they were standing at the railing just two feet in front of me). Another option would be to simply say nothing with the intent of avoiding conflict. This option, however, would be at the potential cost of the peace I was seeking in exchange for fretting and frustration over the apparent lack of manners and respect –on display—pun intended.

Then a third option appeared to me, metaphorically speaking. I came there with the goal of seeking peace. As is often the case in life, something unexpected occurred to disrupt that. Putting this situation into perspective, the ocean was still there. In fact, it was there before they came and would be here long after they left. My "view" still existed, even though I may not have been able to see it completely at the moment. Beyond the shrill voices loudly exchanging drama stories, I could still hear the soothing sound of the waves lapping on the shore. Not a single grain of sand had changed.

I choose to maintain my peace in spite of this distraction, reducing its impact on me to its proper place: a minor, irrelevant, and temporary obstacle in the grand scheme of life. I relaxed to the soft music flowing through my earphones and was thankful I had remembered to bring them. I sank deeper into my chair with the sensation of floating, holding on to my peace. After a while, the visitors left. Whether their behavior was intentional or just oblivious, they took with them what they brought, and I keep my peace. I had won that battle—which in turn multiplied the peace I already possessed.

Proud of myself for that little win, I continued on with the purpose of my visit, which was basking in nature in a peaceful bliss. Right up until the nice gentlemen set up a gas generator in front of me to power the music system for the wedding he was setting up for, which was scheduled to take place soon; it was a lovely wedding. Peace.

SURFS UP

You can't stop the wave's but you can learn to surf. —Jon Kabat-Zinn

Part of mastering the complexity of life is learning how to handle the expected with the unexpected. Ocean waves, while rhythmic, can be unpredictable. A skilled surfer knows to come prepared and understands that it takes time and practice to learn to conquer the waves. They fully expect to be battered and tossed around if they fail to show up with the right equipment or if they don't anticipate there will be some unpredictability. The same is true in life. We seldom can put an end to life's challenges, however, once we come to accept that curve balls will be thrown our way, we are in a better position to navigate the waves of life. When we anticipate and prepare to experience surprises, setbacks, and disappointments, while learning to adapt and recover; we make progress. With the right mindset, riding the waves of life can be an exciting and even enjoyable experience.

Surfs up, ready?

EPILOGUE

During the final stages of writing this book, I felt an overwhelming drive to publish the book on my birth date, September 10. I had thought the sense of urgency was that it would serve as a symbolic re-birth for me, the putting behind of all that I had endured.

The pre-release on September 10th of the advanced reader version was a surreal experience that I will never forget. It wasn't until two days after, however, when a friend informed me that September 10 is World Suicide Prevention Day.

It was then that I realized why I had felt so strongly about that date. I firmly believe that when aligning with our purpose, nothing happens by chance or accident. We will be exactly where we are supposed to be, doing what we are called to do, at the appointed time when we are supposed to.

This experience was powerful and moving for me. I wish the same for everyone seeking to find his or her purpose in the midst of their battle of endurance during a crisis.

A word about the crisis that we bring on ourselves: a self-inflicted crisis.

There is a philosophy that suggests that at the sunset of our lives, when we look back it's not the things we did do that we regret—it's the things we did not do. We hear this repeatedly from interviews conducted with people in the sunset of their lives.

There may be times we regret things we did do; however they most likely will tie back to what we did not do, and that was exercise good judgment.

Other crises we bring on ourselves often relate to matters of principal. People always say they want to hear the truth . . . until they don't like the truth and don't care to hear it. Be prepared to endure the backlash of telling the real truth. Always provide it with dignity, respect, and diplomacy, but always provide it.

These types of crises can be particularly hurtful and challenging because our intent was for a good cause; however, the repercussions that stem from taking the high road can feel devastating. They can impact friendships, relationships, and careers to the point of causing you to not want to tell the truth. Keep telling the truth. Better to be able to walk with your head up during crisis knowing you did the right thing than to suffer even further wondering if the crisis is because you did not.

At the risk of sounding like a hair-club-for-men

infomercial, I'm not just the author, but I have repeatedly leveraged and lived by every word of the coping strategies in this book.

While working on the manuscript for years, I completed it during one of the most difficult times during my life. Not only was I dealing with multiple life crises, but I was also battling health issues that restricted my ability to write. It was all I could do some days to get a few sentences written—on the days I was even able to write. Fighting through intense bouts of depression coupled with debilitating anxiety, I endured and survived by letting go and living in the now on my path to victory.

The preceding chapters are not just concepts, theories, or ideas I've read but practical solutions that I have lived by under tremendous duress. As a result, you may find some of the writing, formatting, or flow untraditional. Know that the birth of this book was in the midst of the type of pain and despair I would not wish on my worst enemies.

Despite all, I was determined that my goal was to give the gift I had been given to give, even if it meant that it would be my parting gift.

In the darkest and toughest moments, when I had reached the bitter end of myself, it was my faith that sustained me.

The Lord is my strength and my shield; My heart trusted in Him, and I am helped; Therefore my heart greatly rejoices, And with my song I will praise Him.
—Psalms 28:7

ACKNOWLEDGMENTS

I would like to thank:

My first round review, editing, and proofing team: my family. Your unconditional support, love, and encouragement are a life-sustaining, priceless gift.

My mom, Bessie, who was my first best friend. She is the very essence of fruits of the spirit and the strongest woman I know. Her balance of intelligence, grace, and strength have taught me to never give up and to be encouraged to stay the course—no matter what.

My dad, Burnie, who led by example in accomplishing many firsts and never accepting being told he could not achieve noble goals.

My sister, Roxane Battle, for inspiring, encouraging, challenging, and believing in me to finally finish and publish this book. I appreciate her willingness to make the sacrifice in publishing her award-winning, bestselling book *Pockets of Joy* to show me that is was possible (smile). I am so very proud of you.

My amazing editor, Candace Johnson, for you invaluable feedback, editing and support in helping make this book something to be proud of.

My friend, Tamara Estepa for your dedication, help,

and support with development, editing and proofing.

Ian Caven, my fellow philosopher, intellectual thought leader, and creative genius who has always been a reliable friend and source of inspiration.

The incredible and strong individuals who provided and allowed me to include their personal stories of tragedies and triumph. I am honored and grateful to have crossed paths. You are my heroes.

All of my other siblings, in-laws, and friends who stood by me encouraged me or simply were willing to lend an ear for me to speak into while refraining from judging or looking down on me as I endured in crisis.

Mrs. Ott, my third-grade teacher, who believed in me and sacrificed her time to help me improving my handwriting.

It was because of all of you that I was able to let go, live now, and win.

ABOUT THE AUTHOR

Nate Battle had been on the verge of becoming a millionaire three different times in his life. However, instead he had to start over from nothing three times. He has endured business failures, layoffs, family crises, corporate upheaval, and battling cancer, and is proud to be a survivor.

Much of the turmoil Nate faced occurred at the same time. There was a point where his career, marriage, finances, and dad were all in the ICU at the same time.

Through these seemingly endless challenges, Nate has endured and learned the art of coping when life gets turned upside down. Experiencing the gut-wrenching pain of hopelessness and despair life can heave on you, he felt the need to share his experience.

He sought to also include the stories of those with whom he crossed paths who stayed the course, didn't quit or give up, and had somehow figured out how to live happily in the midst of the struggle, not just on the other side.

For booking information, contact
Nate at www.natebattle.com

REFERENCES

Leaf, Caroline. *Who Switched Off My Brain? Controlling Toxic Thoughts and Emotions*. Southlake, TX: Iprov, 2009.

Powell, Richard R. *Wabi Sabi Simple: Create Beauty, Value Imperfection, Live Deeply*. Avon, MA: Adams Media, 2005. Print.

Ruiz, Miguel. *The Four Agreements: A Practical Guide to Personal Freedom*. San Rafael, CA: Amber-Allen Pub., 1997.

Tolle, Eckhart. *The Power of Now: A Guide to Spiritual Enlightenment*. Novato, CA: New World Library, 1999. Print.

Dictionary.com, s.v. "crisis," accessed 7 Nov. 2015 http://www.dictionary.com/browse/crisis?s=td.

Dictionary.com, s.v. "endure," accessed 7 Nov. 2015 http://www.dictionary.com/browse/endure?s=t.

Merriam-Webster.com, s.v. "endure," accessed 7 Nov. 2015, http://unabridged.merriam-webster.com/unabridged/endure

Oxford Dictionary.com, s.v. "crisis," accessed 7 Nov. 2015 https://en.oxforddictionaries.com/definition/crisis

Oxford Dictionary.com, s.v. "endure," accessed 7 Nov. 2015, https://en.oxforddictionaries.com/definition/endure

Audiovisual:

Lee, Johnny. *Looking For Love*. Recording. Los Angeles, CA: Full Moon/Asylum: 1980.

Murray, Bill. *St. Vincent*. Film. Directed by Theodore Melfi. Los

Angeles, CA: The Weinstein Company, 2014.